# GREEN
## PASTURES,
## QUIET
## WATERS

# GREEN
# PASTURES,
# QUIET
# WATERS

*Refreshing
Moments from
the Psalms*

## RAY
## PRITCHARD

**MOODY PRESS**
CHICAGO

©1999 by
RAY PRITCHARD

ISBN: 0-8024-8157-4

1 3 5 7 9 10 8 6 4 2
*Printed in the United States of America*

*Dedicated with joy to my brother,*
*Alan Pritchard—*


*Surely you have granted him eternal blessings and made him glad with the joy of your presence.*

Psalm 21:6

# CONTENTS

———— ✳ ————

# ACKNOWLEDGMENTS

———— ✳ ————

Special thanks to Greg Thornton, Jim Bell, Bill Thrasher, and Cheryl Dunlop of Moody Press for many acts of kindness in the writing of this third volume in the trilogy of wisdom books for busy readers. Greg, in particular, has encouraged me in my writing career from the very beginning. Special thanks also to Kathy Duggins and Mia Gale for freeing up my time so I could write. And I continue to be indebted to my wife, Marlene, for her faith, love, and hope, in precisely that order.

# INTRODUCTION

———— ✳ ————

I t is no secret that the book of Psalms is perhaps the most universally beloved book in the Bible. Across the centuries, stretching back thousands of years, people of faith have turned to these ancient hymns for hope, encouragement, direction, and inspiration. The green pastures and quiet waters of the Twenty-third Psalm are familiar to Christians and unbelievers alike. Few have been disappointed in this book of Scripture, because the Psalms look at every part of the soul. Whether you are happy or sad, defeated or triumphant, seeking wisdom or simply needing a way to pour out your soul to God, there is something here for you.

Many years ago I heard Armin Gesswein, a missionary and leader of the prayer movement, say he liked to take "a morning dip in the Psalms." The image of a man swimming in the cool waters has stayed in my mind as a way to understand why this part of the Bible remains so popular. Leviticus is the Word of God too, and so is Nahum, and 2 Peter for that matter, but I don't know anyone who habitually reads those books every morning. But many Christians read the Psalms every day. Some read five a day so that they can finish the book in a month and thus read it through twelve times a year.

So some people read the book dozens of times and a few people read it hundreds of times. Surely there must be something special about a book that never loses its hold over people. It speaks to the human condition. When you read Psalm 23 for the fiftieth time, you find it just as refreshing as the first time you discovered that "The Lord is my shepherd; I shall not want" (KJV).

The book you are holding in your hand is not a commentary on the Psalms. It's too short to be a commentary, and I'm not qualified to write one. Using Armin Gesswein's metaphor, here you have one hundred morning dips in the Psalms. These are short readings (all of them around five hundred words) arranged around ten general topics. My goal in writing this book is to take you into every part of the Psalter. Since there are 150 psalms, I can't cover all of them, or even every verse in each psalm that we will visit. This book is like a tour bus: We don't have time to see everything, but together we'll visit some of the more intriguing sites, and I'll offer some commentary on the passing scenery. I hope when we're done, you'll come back and visit the many nooks and crannies of Psalms left untouched.

I've included a short prayer with each entry as a general way of guiding your response to God. You'll also find three questions for further thought—and possible use in a Bible class or a small group discussion.

As we begin, let's remember that the book of Psalms is first and foremost a hymnbook for the people of God. If we read it without responding in praise, prayer, worship, and confession, then we've missed the reason this book is in the Bible.

One final word: I hope you won't read this book straight through. It's meant to be picked up and read a little bit at a time—an entry here, an entry there, perhaps two or three entries at a time. If you feel like stopping to sing or to pray or to jot down some notes, by all means, put this book aside and spend some time with the Lord. If you want to skip around in the book, that's fine too. My only goal is to lead you into Psalms in a new way and ultimately to meet the One about whom every psalm speaks. If my words help move you in that direction, then our time together will not have been in vain.

*Section One*

# LIFT HIM UP!

*How good it is to sing praises to our God,
how pleasant and fitting to praise him!*
Psalm 147:1

# One

# WORSHIP: THE OIL OF THE SPIRITUAL LIFE

*Worship the Lord in the splendor of his holiness; tremble before him, all the earth.*

Psalm 96:9

My favorite definition of worship comes from William Temple, archbishop of Canterbury many years ago. "To worship is to quicken the conscience by the holiness of God, to feed the mind with the truth of God, to purge the imagination with the beauty of God, to open the heart to the love of God, to devote the will to the purpose of God." Worship is to be the central point of the Christian life, and when we make it first, everything else falls into place.

One fine spring morning in Texas I noticed that the sun was coming out, the grass was beginning to grow, and it was time to bring out the lawn mower. When it wouldn't start I kept pulling until I finally broke the rope. Then I checked the spark plug and put it back in place. I put my fingers in the gas chamber and found dirty gas from the past fall. I checked a few other connections and found everything in working order. The blades were sharp and ready to go—no problem there. I took it to a repair shop, where they said they would fix it. A few days later it was ready. They had had to replace something in the engine. I asked what the matter was. They said there was no oil in the motor. For some reason it had never occurred to me to put oil in a lawn mower. When the oil had run out, the motor wouldn't run anymore.

Behold this simple truth: Worship is the oil of the spiritual life. When you start to run low on worship, your life starts to break down. If you feel a little broken down, it may not be because you are busy, but because you have run low on worship. When you lift the worship of God back to its proper place, your life will start working again.

*Holy God, quicken my heart that I might worship You in spirit and in truth. Amen.*

—— ✳ ——

## A MOMENT'S REFLECTION

Are you "running low" on worship? What do you need to do about it? Take a moment to reread William Temple's definition of worship. Which of those characteristics do you most need in your life right now?

## Two

---

✳

---

# WHERE WORSHIP BEGINS: BOWING BEFORE THE LORD

*Come, let us bow down in worship, let us kneel before the Lord our Maker.*

Psalm 95:6

It has been said that we worship our work, we work at our play, and we play at our worship. In many ways this explains the problem with contemporary Christianity. We worship something, but not the right thing. In all of life nothing is as important as learning how to worship. When we learn how to worship, whole new vistas open before our eyes. Until that happens, our days will be filled with mere religious activity. We will come to church on Sunday morning, we will give money, and we may be very active, but we will miss the one thing for which we were created.

The Westminster Shorter Catechism begins with the following question: "What is the chief end of man?" Answer: "To glorify God and to enjoy him forever." You were created to glorify God in everything, which means that the whole purpose of your life is to honor God in all that you do. That brings us face-to-face with worship.

One of the most common Old Testament words for worship means "to bow down." It has within it the idea of physically bowing down before the Lord. Psalm 95:6 contains two of these ideas: bowing down and kneeling before the Lord. Most of us find that an alien concept since we rarely (if ever) bow down before another person. We might find such an idea odd or even offensive. But true worship means acknowledging God's greatness even to the point of prostrating ourselves on the floor before Him.

The New Testament has a Greek version of that same word, with an additional idea appended to it. One of the central New Testament ideas for worship is to bow down and to kiss the ground. What does that tell us about worship? It tells us that worship is the response of the believer to the greatness, majesty, and magnificence of God. Worship means to declare God's worth. It is to give God the honor that is due Him. It is to render to God the glory that attaches to His position as King of the universe. If you want to say it in a very modern way, it is to pay God the ultimate compliment of treating God as God—and as nothing less than God. This is where all worship must begin.

*Eternal God, You alone are worthy of all praise. May I see You as You truly are: the one, true, and eternal God before whom all creation will one day bow. Amen.*

## A MOMENT'S REFLECTION

Under what circumstances would you bow before another person? Have you ever bowed in worship before the Lord? Why is the physical act of bowing (or kneeling) important in our worship?

*Three*

---

# ADORATION:
# IT INVOLVES ALL
# THAT YOU HAVE

*Clap your hands, all you nations; shout to God with cries of joy.*

Psalm 47:1

Worship is to be the central act of life. Since it is supposed to be the main thing we do, worship is not simply coming to church. It is something we actively do with our bodies and entire selves. The Bible mentions things like singing, clapping, shouting, laughing, kneeling, saying "amen," speaking, sitting in silence, chanting, praying, lifting up the hands, lying prostrate on the floor, beating the chest, crying, blessing God and others, joining hands, singing in the choir, listening to the choir, playing cymbals, horns, bells, pipes, trumpets, and even dancing. This tells us that worship is to involve the whole person in every area of life. Please get it out of your mind that worship only happens at 11:00 on Sunday morning. What happens at that time is the corporate gathering together of the body of Christ, but worshiping God touches your entire life seven days a week.

Warren Wiersbe defines worship as "the believer's adoring response of all that he is, mind, emotions, will and body, to all that God is and says and does." I find that to be a profound statement. That definition doesn't mention a pipe organ or a contemporary praise band. It doesn't say anything about drums or a robed choir. Nor does it touch the burning issue of choruses versus stately hymns. We get hung up on those outward manifestations when the Bible is telling us that worship involves our response of all that we are to all that God has revealed Himself to be.

That will be manifested in many different ways in your life. Certainly Sunday morning is going to be important, but if the only time you worship is on Sunday morning, you have missed what the Bible has to say about worship. When God Himself grips your soul, every day will be Sunday, and worship will be as natural as breathing.

*Lord God, teach me to worship with all my heart and all my soul all the time. Amen.*

## A MOMENT'S REFLECTION

How do you define worship? Do you find it easier to worship in church on Sunday morning than during the week? How would today be different if you worshiped God all day long?

*Four*

---✳---

# WHOLEHEARTED WORSHIP: PRACTICAL WAYS TO PUT GOD FIRST

*I will praise you, O Lord, with all my heart; I will tell of all your wonders.*

Psalm 9:1

If worship is going to be important, then preparation for worship will become very important. Consider a typical Sunday morning routine. You get up, fix and eat breakfast, shave or put on your makeup, fix your hair, iron your clothes, put on your dress or your coat and tie, pile the kids in the car, and barely make it to the service. How much time did you spend preparing your heart for the worship of God? You had to get your face ready—what about your heart? You think you had to iron your pants, but did you take time to iron the wrinkles out of your soul?

How do you think God feels when He paid the price of His Son's blood and His people come in late and unprepared to worship Him?

Your attitude changes how you come to worship. You will come eagerly, joyfully, expectantly. All too often our hearts are not in it. We sing "There Is a Redeemer" (*I wonder how the Bulls are going to do today?*); "Great Is the

Lord" (*It sure is getting hot in here*), "When We All Get to Heaven" (*I wonder if I should put my money in the stock market?*) We come distracted; we come busy, hurried, and worried. Maybe we come angry. I am convinced that the devil stirs up trouble in Christian families on Sunday morning so he can distract their hearts from worshiping God.

Worshiping with a whole heart means that we lay aside a critical spirit and join with God's people in praising the Lord. If Jesus is to be the Lord, then worship must have priority. What is the first and greatest commandment? "You shall love the Lord your God with all your heart, all your soul, all your mind and all your strength, then your neighbor as yourself." It is not church work first and then worship. It is worshiping God and loving Him first, and out of that flows everything else.

*Lord, help me to worship You with a whole heart today. Amen.*

## A MOMENT'S REFLECTION

How much time did you spend preparing your heart for worship last Sunday? Name the worries and concerns that keep you from focusing on God right now. Spend a few moments giving those things to the Lord.

------ ✳ ------

# Five

# FEAR AND TREMBLING:
# A HEALTHY RESPECT
# FOR WHO GOD IS

*Serve the Lord with fear and rejoice with trembling.*
                                                    Psalm 2:11

Rejoicing and trembling may seem like opposite emotions, but the psalmist joins them together as the proper way to approach God. We are to rejoice that we know the Lord but we are never, ever to take Him lightly. As Charles Spurgeon says, this is a "sacred compound." Fear without joy is torment, and joy without fear is presumption. Martin Luther pointed out that hypocrites rejoice in God without fear because they have too high an opinion of themselves. But the righteous despair of themselves (thus they tremble); casting themselves upon God, they rejoice in His mercy. True believers constantly accuse themselves (in the sense of being deeply aware of their own sinfulness) and at the same time constantly rejoice in God their Savior. They are like wheat when the husk of self-trust is broken off, leaving only the sweet fruit of Christ within.

The word trembling carries with it the concept of timidity and fear—which in itself might seem to contradict the invitation to "come boldly" to the throne of grace

(Hebrews 4:16 KJV). We are invited to come to God as often as we like—especially in the "time of need"—but we must not come lightly or flippantly or casually. We are to tremble in the presence of the Lord, to feel such gratitude for the awesome privilege of knowing Him that we come into His presence knowing that we are standing before the King of the universe.

If that thought doesn't make you fearful, it should. It is the sudden fear that grips you late at night when you are almost asleep, right on the edge, and suddenly you hear a tiny noise, a strange sound, and you think, *Burglars have broken in.* It happens to me from time to time. I'll be drifting off to sleep when I hear something creak. All at once I'm wide awake, sitting up in bed, straining to hear every sound. One writer called it "aroused fear in the moment of danger." Serve God that way so you can hear everything He is saying to you in the Word. It keeps you on your toes.

Worship is serious business. Don't take it lightly. Don't drift away from the Lord. Stay on your toes. Be alert.

This warning is well taken, because it's easy to go to church and just tune out. It's easy to read the Bible and pay no attention to the message. It's easy to take God for granted and be careless about things that are really deadly serious.

*O God of all things, help me not to take lightly that which You take seriously. Amen.*

28

—✳—

## A MOMENT'S REFLECTION

Have you ever trembled over your own sin? How can such self-despair lead on to rejoicing? What can we do to keep from taking God lightly?

---

*

# Six

# GLORIFY GOD: ENHANCING GOD'S REPUTATION IN THE WORLD

*Glorify the Lord with me; let us exalt his name together.*

Psalm 34:3

What precisely does it mean to glorify God? The particular word translated "glorify" in this verse is sometimes translated by words such as "magnify," "exalt," "pile high," and "make grow." It has within it the concept of increasing the size of something. In this context it means to recognize who God really is and to honor Him for what He has done. You glorify someone when you recognize his true identity and the true worth of his accomplishments.

When our boys were young, we took them on a short vacation to visit relatives in Lexington, Kentucky. During an afternoon trip to a miniature golf course, we noticed an older gentleman with his grandchildren on another part of the course. "Do you know who that is?" someone asked. We didn't. "He was the governor of Kentucky." "You're just making that up." But it was true. The older gentleman turned out to be a distinguished former governor of Kentucky. Our opinion changed instantly from disinterest to great respect.

The most common Old Testament word for glory means to treat something as heavy or weighty in nature. The word was used in Genesis 31 for animals heavy-laden with gold. The word also refers to the shining light of God's presence. That glory was the cloud by day and the fiery pillar by night that led the people of God through the wilderness. Later it was the light that filled the tabernacle and the temple. Exodus 24:17 tells us that God's glory was like a consuming fire on the top of Mount Sinai. Thomas Watson, the great Puritan preacher, called glory "the sparkling of Deity."

When we pass into the New Testament we meet a Greek word, *doxa*, from which we get the English word doxology. This word has the idea of honor, dignity, and reputation. That last word—reputation—brings us very close to the meaning of "glory" in Psalm 34:3. I remember hearing Dr. Charles Ryrie explain that God's glory is His reputation in the world. To live for God's glory means to live so that God's reputation is enhanced, not diminished.

That leads me to an important thought. In one sense you cannot diminish God's glory. It exists forever because God is eternal. To paraphrase C. S. Lewis, you cannot diminish God's glory any more than a madman can diminish the sun merely by scribbling "darkness" on the walls on his cell. However, you can cause others to see the glory of God or to dismiss it entirely by the personal choices you make every day.

God's purpose for you and me is that we would glorify Him by recognizing in our daily lives who He is and what great things He has done for us. As we do that, His reputation is enhanced in the world.

*Lord Jesus, I pray to be the kind of person who makes it easy for others to believe in You. Amen.*

— ✳ —

## A MOMENT'S REFLECTION

Why did God leave His earthly reputation in the hands of His children? What difference does that make for you? Name three practical ways you can glorify God this week.

---

✳

---

# Seven

# WHY DID THIS HAPPEN? PONDER THE MYSTERIOUS WAYS OF GOD

*All mankind will fear; they will proclaim the works of God and ponder what he has done.*

Psalm 64:9

For four years a young couple tried to have a baby. After many expensive infertility treatments, the wife conceived and gave birth to a healthy baby girl. This is what the new father had to say:

> I've been reflecting on my life a lot lately. I guess that's pretty normal for a new dad. If a newborn can't blow away the dross of life I don't know what can. There is nothing worse than helplessly watching a loved one struggle and suffer . . . on the flipside there's nothing like watching Mama with her newborn child. In the elation of having prayer answered so perfectly I have to say that I fear God today more than ever.

He went on to say that he has tried to avoid the temptation of turning into God's cheerleader just because it worked out the way they wanted. When things work out well, it's all too easy to draw conclusions about why

God acted in a certain way. "It didn't strike me as too genuine to take a four-year roller-coaster ride and sum it up neatly in two sentences of 'God's reasoning' for why it happened the way it did."

He spoke of the miscarriages they had suffered and the grief group they attended. "I've been through some tough times before, but that was dark. I don't think I said a sincere prayer for six months after that." He had no answers for himself—or for the others in the group. When the baby finally came, he asked himself a hard question:

> What separates us from the rest of the group? We have a beautiful girl, the answer we wanted, and others are still suffering. Certainly we've done nothing to merit it. All I know is that we conceived a child in between infertility treatments, something the doctor said was statistically improbable, and the pregnancy went to term and the baby girl is just adorable. And nobody can lay claim to the glory but God alone. I know He is God. And I fear Him because He has all the keys. The fine line between bitter and sweet is entirely up to Him. Whether I get joy or sorrow, He is still God and I can't live apart from Him so I have to trust Him and walk with Him no matter what. I think I have as much faith as I used to. It's just tempered, not so wide eyed, but it's certainly more reverent. I never used to truly understand the "fear God" stuff in the Old Testament. I think I'm beginning to today.

No one can understand what God does. Ponder His ways. Proclaim His power. Bow down and worship Him.

*Almighty God, Your ways are beyond finding out. Keep alive in me a conscious wonder as I consider the things You have done. Amen.*

———✳———

## A MOMENT'S REFLECTION

In what ways can answered prayer be just as mysterious as unanswered prayer? What happens when we try to explain the unexplainable acts of God? Which side of the bitter/sweet line are you on right now?

---
*

# Eight

# THE SANCTUARY: WHERE GOD ANSWERS HARD QUESTIONS

*When I tried to understand all this, it was oppressive to me till I entered the sanctuary of God; then I understood their final destiny.*

Psalm 73:16–17

P salm 73 has been a personal favorite for as long as I have been reading the psalms. Written by Asaph (leader of one of the temple choirs), it deals with a question that has troubled the people of God across the centuries: Why do the wicked prosper? He is not asking why the righteous suffer (as Job does), but his eyes are fixed on a more perplexing problem. If God is a God of moral justice, how can He allow wicked men to prosper in their wickedness? Why doesn't He judge them? Why do they seem to "get away with it"?

Why do pornographers make millions? Why do presidents lie under oath and see their poll numbers go up? Why do deadbeat dads flee from their responsibilities while single moms toil to pay the bills? Why do murderers get off the hook and end up signing book deals instead of going to prison? Why are cutthroat corporate leaders given huge bonuses each year? On and on the list goes.

Asaph had pondered these questions deeply, and the answers he received troubled him. In fact, his foothold in faith had almost slipped as he envied the arrogance of the wicked (vv. 2–3). Ah, arrogance. That's part of the conundrum. It's not just that the wicked prosper. That much we might be able to swallow. But it's their swaggering unconcern for anyone else, their boasting about how they did it, their bragging to their friends that crime really does pay. Either they think God doesn't know or God doesn't care, or maybe God is on their side (v. 11). O Lord, why do You allow such men to prosper? Why don't You strike them dead?

Worst of all, it makes the righteous feel as if we have kept our hands pure in vain. Why bother keeping the rules if the bad guys win by breaking the rules? Where is the reward for doing right?

The answer came in a strange way. Asaph went to the sanctuary of God to pray and to worship. There he encountered the God who stands above the teeming ways of humanity. There he learned again that "though the wheels of God grind slowly, they grind exceeding small." In the words of Martin Luther King Jr. he learned that "the arm of the universe is long, but it bends toward justice."

Justice! That's the answer. The wicked prosper in this life because they are about to suffer for all eternity. They will soon be swept away by terrors they cannot begin to imagine (v. 19).

Are you tempted to doubt God's plan? Do you sometimes wonder if the wrong team will win in the end? Do not despair. Go back to God's house. Enter His sanctuary. Dwell with His people. Let worship lead you to the truth. Those who serve God in this life will never regret it in the life to come.

*O God, I see many things that confuse me and many things that make no sense at all. Forgive me when I doubt Your wisdom. Restore my confidence in Your eternal plan. Amen.*

——✳——

## A MOMENT'S REFLECTION

Name three ways you see the wicked prospering. Why doesn't God judge them right now? What does it mean to you to "go to the sanctuary" of God?

---

✳

---

# Nine

# UNITED PRAYER: THE CHURCH'S SECRET WEAPON

*Glory in his holy name; let the hearts of those who seek the Lord rejoice.*

Psalm 105:3

"Prayer is not everything but everything is by prayer." So said Ray Ortlund. All Christians would agree with that statement. No matter what our background, instinctively we know that prayer is central to the Christian life.

You are probably familiar with Corrie ten Boom, whose family hid Jews in Holland during World War II. After being released from the Ravensbruck Concentration Camp near the end of the war, she had a vital ministry for Christ around the world for four decades. Her story is told in the book and the movie *The Hiding Place*. How important is prayer? Let Corrie ten Boom answer that question: "When a Christian shuns fellowship with other Christians, the devil smiles. When he stops reading the Bible, the devil laughs. When he stops praying, the devil shouts for joy."

In the last several years a number of important books

have been written on the thesis that we are on the brink of a great worldwide revival. Many people who say that believe that this revival will be the last great move of the Spirit before Jesus returns to the earth. Of the many signs of revival around the world, none is more important than this: There is a growing movement of prayer greater than anything in Christian history, a movement that spans the continents and the denominations, bringing together the people of God as never before.

A friend called recently and told me that he had visited the Brooklyn Tabernacle, a church with a dynamic ministry in a very difficult urban setting. Each week the church ministers to eight to ten thousand people. It has excellent Bible teaching, great music, warm fellowship. But my friend reported that the Tuesday night prayer meeting draws the largest crowd each week. No wonder the church is growing.

Some years ago during a visit to a mission station in Belize, God impressed on my heart that if the church I pastor was going to go to the next level, we would only get there through prayer. The Lord clearly said that we wouldn't get there by preaching, programs, or publicity. Prayer must be the key.

That seems elementary, doesn't it? What pastor wouldn't say that, and what church doesn't believe it? Let us therefore repeat it once again—prayer is the key. Acts 2:42 tells us that the early disciples "devoted themselves to . . . prayer." Is it any wonder that as a result God gave them unity, miracles, and thousands of people coming to Christ? All things are possible when a church prays.

*Lord Jesus, may my church become a house of prayer—*
*and grant that I might become a praying Christian.*
*Amen.*

———— ✳ ————

## A MOMENT'S REFLECTION

What place does prayer have in your own church? Why is
united prayer so important? Name three good things that
happen when believers pray together.

*Ten*

---
✳
---

# UNIVERSAL WORSHIP: GOD'S DESIRE FOR THE NATIONS

*Praise the Lord, all you nations; extol him, all you peoples.*
Psalm 117:1

Praise is the universal language of the Christian church. Go anywhere around the world and you will discover how true this is. In my years of traveling I have raised my hands in charismatic worship in Belize and I have worshiped in a tiny Russian church not far from the Volga River. Although the only words of Russian I knew were "Good morning" and "Yes" and "No," when the believers stood to sing the Lord's Prayer, I stood and sang along with them.

During my last tour of the Holy Land, our group spent one Sunday night at the King of Kings congregation that meets in the Jerusalem YMCA. Many of the choruses were in Hebrew, yet we joined right in and worshiped God with our brothers and sisters. The same thing happened during an evangelistic crusade in Pignon, Haiti. When those dear brothers and sisters sang "Great Is Thy Faithfulness" in Creole, we sang along in English.

Recently I worshiped in several Nigerian churches.

Sometimes we all sang in English and sometimes they sang hymns in Hausa and I sang along in English. I have sung "Just As I Am" with forty-five thuosand others at a Billy Graham Crusade in Denver, listened with awe to the magnificent sound of "Holy, Holy, Holy" on a pipe organ, stood around a campfire in Schroon Lake, New York, with three hundred teenagers singing "We Are Climbing Jacob's Ladder," heard the beautiful chanting of the Catholic monks at the Church of the Holy Sepulchre in Jerusalem, and attended an Orthodox liturgy in St. Petersburg, Russia. On a trip to Paraguay my wife and I learned to sing "Hay Vida" in Spanish and one or two songs in the Guarani language.

I have been in churches where the music was fast, slow, and in-between, in formal liturgies and informal testimony services, in churches that followed the church year, and in churches that had never heard of the church year. When we get to heaven, we will all praise the Lamb together—redeemed saints from every nation, tongue, tribe, race, culture, and ethnic group on the face of the earth. We will together bow the knee before the mighty Son of God and declare Him worthy of honor, praise, power, glory, wisdom, and adoration.

Together we will worship Him in unending praise around the throne of God. In that day it won't be one style or language over another. It will simply be heavenly praise to Jesus. What a wonderful day that will be.

Until then we will worship Him in different ways, but if those ways are acceptable to God they must be acceptable to us also. In that spirit let us move forward with joy, with enthusiasm, with excitement, not judging each other or putting each other down, but celebrating the fact that we are still one church, one body, one family of God. We're not all alike, but we are one people.

*Lord Jesus, hasten the day when all Your children will worship You with one voice around the throne of God. Amen.*

——✳——

## A MOMENT'S REFLECTION

Make your own list of the different worship experiences you have had. What does that teach you about God's intention for His people? Why do we argue about worship styles?

*Section Two*
# OUR AWESOME GOD

*But you, O Lord, sit enthroned forever; your
renown endures through all generations.*
Psalm 102:12

---
✳
---

# Eleven

# KNOWING GOD: THE CHRISTIAN'S SPECIAL PRIVILEGE

*In Judah God is known; his name is great in Israel.*

Psalm 76:1

The entire message of the Christian faith comes down to this: Through Jesus Christ we can know God personally and intimately. This is an astonishing thing to say. Can anyone truly say, "I know God" and not be boasting? Yes. If we are not astonished by that, it's because we take it too much for granted.

Every year the newspaper publishes a list of the most admired men and women in America. And each year I scan the list to see if I know anyone on it. So far the answer has always been in the negative. But I can truly say, "I know God" because I met Him when I met Jesus Christ. How can that be? How can one man's death— good as it may be—introduce me to God? Dead is dead. How can His death do that? I'll tell you how. He's not dead anymore.

You see, if His death had been no more than our death, He would still be dead. His death did what our death could never do—it paid for the sins of the world. Therefore, God raised Him from the dead.

Several years ago when my wife and I visited Jerusalem, we toured the holy places. Our guide took us outside the Damascus gate north of the city to a place called Gordon's Calvary. Erosion has carved the image of a skull in a limestone cliff. Next to it is a lovely tomb in a peaceful Middle Eastern garden. Many people think this is the spot where Jesus rose from the dead.

Because the opening is very small, I had to duck to go inside. For a few seconds, I saw nothing until my eyes adjusted to the darkness. Then I could easily make out the two chambers. Visitors stand in the mourners chamber. A wrought-iron fence protects the chamber where the body was laid. As I looked around the burial chamber, I could see faint markings left by Christian pilgrims from earlier centuries. There is no body to be found in this tomb. Whoever was buried there evidently left a long time ago. The Garden Tomb is empty.

As I exited back into the sunlight, my eyes fastened upon a wooden sign: "Why seek ye the living among the dead? He is not here, but he is risen" (Luke 24:5–6 KJV).

I'm sure and certain that Jesus is alive. I've read it in the pages of God's book. I've experienced Him in my own life. Jesus is alive today. His resurrection proves that His death had infinite value. And through Him I know God. Through Him I believe in God. Through Him my faith and my hope are in God. That's the astonishing privilege: Through the redeeming death and victorious resurrection of Jesus Christ, we can know God.

*Lord God, You are the source of all knowing, and the greatest knowledge of all is to know You. Thank You for revealing Yourself in the person of Your Son, the Lord Jesus Christ, my Savior. Amen.*

—— ✳ ——

## A MOMENT'S REFLECTION

What do Christians mean when we say that we know God? How does the resurrection of Jesus relate to that truth? How do you know that Jesus rose from the dead?

---
✷
---

# Twelve

# UNFAILING LOVE: WHY JESUS WENT TO THE CROSS

*How priceless is your unfailing love! Both high and low among men find refuge in the shadow of your wings.*

Psalm 36:7

The concept of unfailing love sounds attractive, doesn't it? Think of a world in which promises are always kept and the good of others rules every personal relationship. Such a world seems like a dream when compared to this poor fallen world of broken promises and broken hearts. No wonder the psalmist called God's unfailing love "priceless." How much we all long for that kind of love—and how much we would gladly pay to experience it.

What we long for, God has provided in the gift of His Son, the Lord Jesus Christ. This is the "indescribable" gift of 2 Corinthians 9:15, the final proof of God's loving nature. Because God so loved the world, He sent Jesus to be our Savior.

But that raises a profound question: How did Jesus love the world He came to save? How was His love demonstrated? The answer goes something like this. He loved the world with total vulnerability. He gave Himself so completely that the world turned against Him. He loved the world so much that He was beaten, mocked, bruised, abused, hated, reviled, slandered, and insulted. In the end, the very world He came to save turned against Him. Finally, they nailed Him to the cross.

We know that. We've heard it for years. But there's a deeper point here. Jesus had the power to stop people from hurting Him, and He chose not to use it. He didn't have to take the abuse. He didn't have to allow the mockery. As the song says, "He could have called ten thousand angels to destroy the world and set Him free." That was His prerogative. He was the Son of God. All the power of the universe was at His disposal. One word and a legion of angels would be dispatched to His aid.

But He chose not to do it. That's how He loved the world—with total vulnerability. He loved the world so much He was willing to be killed for the world He loved. The Pharisees thought they had outwitted Him, but they could do nothing without His willing consent.

"Go ahead. Spit on Me. Curse Me. Mock Me. Beat Me. Kill Me. Do what you wish. But I still love you. Nothing you can do can make Me stop loving you."

How does Jesus love us? With total, self-sacrificing, vulnerable, unfailing love. No wonder men and women find refuge under the wings of a God who can love like that.

*O Lord, how magnificent is Your love toward me. Thank You for loving me when I was still a sinner and far from You. Amen.*

—✳—

## A MOMENT'S REFLECTION

In what way does Jesus "prove" the unfailing love of God?
Why didn't Jesus use the power at His disposal to come
down from the cross? What does that tell you about the
nature of His love?

*Thirteen*

———— ✳ ————

# OMNIPOTENCE:
# HE DOES WHATEVER
# PLEASES HIM

*Our God is in heaven; he does whatever pleases him.*

Psalm 115:3

The word omnipotence means "all-powerful" and refers to the fact that God's power is infinite and unlimited. He can do with power anything that power can do. Said another way, God has the power to do all He wills to do. He has both the resources and the ability to work His will in every circumstance. If you prefer a simpler definition, just think of these three words: "God is able." That's what omnipotence means. He is able to do everything He needs to do or wants to do.

This doctrine is everywhere assumed in the Bible. One might easily find five hundred verses that either teach omnipotence or implicitly assume it. As a simple summary statement we may say that there are no limits to what God can do because there are no limits to God.

Among the many titles given to God in the Old Testament is one that relates directly to His omnipotence. In Genesis 17:1 God spoke to ninety-nine-year-old Abraham, to whom He had promised a child. By this time his body was "as good as dead" (see Romans 4:19–22). In the face of all his very understandable doubts, God reassured him by calling Himself El Shaddai, which means almighty God. It was God's way of saying, "Don't look in the mirror, Abraham. Look at Me. If I say you're going to have a son, it's going to happen. Age means nothing to Me. I am almighty God."

If our God is good and if He cares for us, then we can believe He has all power, even in the face of sickness, suffering, and death itself. During my twenty-one years as a pastor, I have discovered that a person's starting point makes all the difference. If you start with your trials and try to reason back to God, you'll never make it. Start with lung cancer and it's hard to find God. Start with divorce and it's hard to find God. Start with rape and it's hard to find God. Start with bankruptcy and it's hard to find God. He's there, but He's hard to see when you start with your own difficulty.

You've got to start with God and reason from what you know about God back to your trials. An invisible line stretches from God to us. That line is the line of God's goodness. We rest our faith on that invisible line. That's why 2 Corinthians 4:18 says that "we fix our eyes not on what is seen, but on what is unseen." As long as you start with what you see around you, you'll have a hard time finding God in the darkest moments of life. But if you start with God, His light will illumine your darkness.

*Almighty God, increase my faith so that I might believe without wavering that You are greater than all my problems. Amen.*

—✳—

## A MOMENT'S REFLECTION

How do you know that "God is able" to meet your needs? In times of difficulty, why is your starting point all important? Take a moment to thank God for His mighty power.

------------ * ------------

# Fourteen

# GOD WITH US: FACING THE IMPOSSIBILITIES OF LIFE

*Even though I walk through the valley of the shadow of death, I will fear no evil, for you are with me.*

Psalm 23:4

Let's suppose that one day as you are walking down the street, you see a huge man coming toward you. Let's suppose he's really big—at least thirty-five feet tall. Let's say he weighs in at about 1,500 pounds, all muscle. And he's bearing down on you. As you consider the situation, only one question comes into your mind: Do I know this man? If you don't, it's time to start running in the opposite direction. But if you know him, you wait till he comes up to you, you smile, he smiles and greets you, and together you walk side by side down the street. If you know that man, you're going to stay close by his side and fear nothing at all.

That's why Psalm 23:4 says, "I will fear no evil, for you are with me." If God is walking by your side, you have nothing to fear.

The omnipotence of God is thus a doctrine of wonderful comfort to the believer. The all-powerful God is with me. He exercises His power on my behalf. Whenever I need Him, and even when I think I don't, He is there.

He never fails. All His plans for me will come to pass. I can trust Him completely.

First Corinthians 1:23–24 tells us that the preaching of the Cross is foolishness to the world, but to those who are being saved it is the power of God. To the world the Cross was a terrible waste, a tragedy, an enormous mistake. But to those who believe, it is a demonstration of the power of God.

Think about that for a moment. In the very place where God seemed to be defeated, there we see God's power. Is the all-powerful God good, and does He care for us? Look to the bloody Cross and judge for yourself.

He who had all power gave it up and became weak like us. He knows what it is to die young and be cut off in the midst of life. When we come to the Cross, we come weak, confused, broken, perplexed, bruised, anxious, and frustrated. And there at the Cross, in that place where the world sees weakness, there we find the power of God. We come helpless to the God who is our help and weak to the God who is our strength.

If God were not omnipotent, Jesus would still be dead. But if God can raise the dead, He can do anything. Let that thought encourage you this week as you face the impossibilities of life. Just remember, you're not alone, for almighty God walks by your side.

*Almighty God, I will not fear as long as You are walking next to me. Please remind me of this the next time I am afraid. Amen.*

56

—✳—

## A MOMENT'S REFLECTION

Name three ways that God's omnipotence is a comfort to the believer. Why does the world think the Cross was foolishness? How does the Cross demonstrate God's unlimited power?

---

✳

# Fifteen

# OMNISCIENCE: HIS EYE IS ON THE SPARROW

*You know when I sit and when I rise; you perceive my thoughts from afar.*

Psalm 139:2

It has been said that God's omniscience is a comfort to believers and a terror to unbelievers. The comfort is easy to see. If He truly knows all things and if He ordains all things, then everything that happens to me or to those I love must happen as part of His plan. F. B Meyer has written, "It is in proportion as we see God's will in the various events of life and surrender ourselves either to bear it or do it, that we shall find earth's bitter circumstances becoming sweet and its hard things easy."

I received a message this week from someone who had never written me before. This person's family is going through a terribly difficult time and there is no end in sight. The trial may continue for some time to come. This is what she had to say:

> I have known the truth of Romans 8:28 in my head for many years, but only over the last month have the words had a meaning for my heart. I am convinced

that this whole situation has a purpose, but I am still struggling with the "What." Without the promises of God, I am sure that I would be unable to carry on, going to work and supporting my kids.

If this letter sounds disjointed, it is just how my thoughts have been over the past several weeks. But I have continued to hold on to something you wrote in your book . . . (to paraphrase) Don't worry about 2 or 3 weeks from now, because God has already been there. I know that He continues to hold our entire family in the palm of His hand and that He is directing this to its own end and to His glory. I know that since He cares for the sparrows, He surely is caring for us.

That's a wonderful statement by a believer who, though struggling to understand her own situation, has rested her faith on the fact of God's sovereignty over the details of life. Somewhere I ran across a wonderful statement of what sovereignty really means. God's sovereignty means "He knows what He is doing, and He is doing it." That sums it up, doesn't it?

Although Andrew Murray lived almost one hundred years ago, many of his books are still in print, including the classic *With Christ in the School of Prayer*. During a low period in his own life, he wrote the following words: "He brought me here. He will keep me here. He will make this trial a blessing. He will bring me out again. Therefore, I am here by God's appointment, in His keeping, under His training, for His time."

We often hear it said that "disappointment is His appointment." But that can only be true if God is in charge of the details of life.

> *Thank You, Father, for putting me right where I am today. I am confident that I am here by Your appointment and not by chance or circumstance. Amen.*

—— ✳ ——

## A MOMENT'S REFLECTION

In what sense does God "ordain" everything that comes to pass? How have you recently seen God at work in the details of your own life? Before going on, take a moment to read the Andrew Murray quote out loud.

———— ✳ ————

# Sixteen

# OMNIPRESENCE: HERE, THERE, AND EVERYWHERE

*Where can I go from your Spirit? Where can I flee from your presence?*

Psalm 139:7

The doctrine of God's omnipresence means that God is everywhere present at all times. This truth has several important implications. *First, God cannot be contained in a building.* Sometimes I hear well-meaning people call the church the "house of God," as if His presence somehow specially dwells in a building made by the hands of man. But a church is not a holy place in the sense that the temple was a holy place. Today God dwells among His people and in His people wherever they are and wherever they go.

*Second, He is always present, whether we believe it or not.* In the early days of space travel one of the Russian cosmonauts returned from orbiting the earth to announce that he had looked out his space capsule and had not seen God anywhere. Dr. W. A. Criswell of the First Baptist Church of Dallas replied, "Let him take off his space suit for just one second and he'll see God quick enough."

*Third, He is present even in the worst moments of life.* God's omnipresence means that He is there in the midst of suffering, pain, sickness, sorrow, anger, grief, bitterness, divorce, betrayal, murder, rape, sexual abuse, cancer, AIDS, abortion, warfare, famine, earthquakes, fires, floods, every natural disaster, accidents, personal loss, and at the moment of death.

*Fourth, He is always available to us wherever we go, twenty-four hours a day.* Can you imagine what it would be like if we prayed only to have a angel tell us, "I'm sorry, but God is busy handling a major crisis in the Middle East. Leave your name and number and someone will get back to you as soon as possible"? That will never happen, because all of God is completely available to you no matter where you are. Though there be a thousand wars in a thousand places, our God hears you as if you were the only one praying.

*Fifth, we may rely fully on Him no matter how desperate our situation may be.* Recently I spoke with two elderly Christian women. One had just been diagnosed with cancer. When I talked with her, she said, "Pastor, don't worry about me. The Lord has been so good to me." She's eighty years old. Later I spoke with a woman who is ninety, very weak and frail and eager to go to heaven. Her voice quivered, but her faith was strong. "I'm just trusting in the Lord," she told me. These dear saints have learned through a lifetime of walking with God that He will never leave them, for He is always present with His people.

*Father, thank You for being there whenever we need You and for being there even when we don't sense Your presence. Amen.*

## A MOMENT'S REFLECTION

Define God's omnipresence. How does this truth apply to your prayer life? According to 1 Corinthians 6:19–20, where is God's temple today?

---
✳
---

# Seventeen

# GOD OUR SHEPHERD: GOOD NEWS FOR WAYWARD SHEEP

*He makes me lie down in green pastures, he leads me beside quiet waters, he restores my soul.*

Psalm 23:2–3a

Matthew Henry commented that Psalm 23 has been sung by Christians everywhere, "and will be while the world stands, with a great deal of pleasure and satisfaction." Those words still ring true three hundred years later. The Twenty-third Psalm may well be the most familiar passage in the Bible. Our children learn it by heart almost from the time they know how to read. It is the psalm for every season of life.

"Shepherd" may seem a homely name for God, yet it reveals an essential part of His character. All that a shepherd does to protect and provide for his sheep, the Lord does for His children. The present tense of the first verse is crucial. The Lord *is* my Shepherd—not just that He *was*, nor that He *will be* in the distant future. Friends come and go, even beloved family members die, but the eternal God is our eternal Shepherd—today, tomorrow, and forever.

Verse 2 contains two lovely pictures of the shepherd's care of his sheep. First, he provides rest: "he makes me lie down in green pastures." The flock needs a safe place to rest, and the shepherd must find it, because the sheep can't do it on their own. So the shepherd searches out a lush meadow filled with green grass, not hot desert or rocky soil. There the hungry sheep feed, and there they rest before moving on.

Second, there is refreshment: "He leads me beside quiet waters." Literally, "waters of resting places," speaking of an oasis in the desert. The shepherd knows where the water is, and he leads the sheep to water because they would never find it on their own.

Rest and refreshment lead to restoration: "He restores my soul." The word restore has within it the idea of returning a thing to its original condition. Here it means that the Lord will provide everything I need so that my soul will hunger and thirst no more. As a good meal at the end of a hard day restores the body, so the Lord "restores" the soul of those who trust in Him. If it is true that "we all, like sheep, have gone astray" (Isaiah 53:6), it is also true that the Lord Himself restores us. The Shepherd comes to where we have fallen, bends over us, encourages us, picks us up, and carries us safely home again. And He does it every time I lose my way. It is because the Lord restores my soul again and again that I am going to dwell in the house of the Lord forever.

God promises to do all this for those who follow Him. Right now we're on a journey, a pilgrimage from earth to heaven. We're on our way home. The road may seem long and lonely. Fear not, child of God. If the Lord is your Shepherd, you have everything you need—now and forever.

> *Father, You have provided all I need and more besides. Thank You for an overabundance of grace, because I feel like I'm going to need it all today. Amen.*

—✳—

### A MOMENT'S REFLECTION

Have you ever memorized Psalm 23? If not, take a few moments to read it aloud several times. Then write it out phrase by phrase—adding your own personal words of application. How has the Lord "restored" your soul recently?

———— ✳ ————

# Eighteen

# GOD'S WRATH: A FORGOTTEN DOCTRINE

*The Lord is at your right hand; he will crush kings on the day of his wrath.*

Psalm 110:5

I t's the word wrath that grabs our attention. We're accustomed to hearing about the love of God. We know about the grace of God. We sing about the mercy of God. We extol the glory of God. We ponder the holiness of God. But the wrath of God? We hardly ever mention it. There aren't many hymns about God's wrath. We'd much rather sing "Jesus loves me, this I know."

The reasons for this apparent neglect are not hard to find. Most of us would rather hear about love and grace. I know I would rather preach about God's grace. After all, to speak of the wrath of God makes us appear narrow-minded and judgmental. And on another level, God's wrath is difficult to comprehend, so in some ways this is a doctrine that is easy to overlook. The thought that nice people we know might someday go to eternal hell is so overwhelming—and so disheartening—that we'd much rather not think about it at all.

Many Christians feel as if they have to apologize for this doctrine. Some think it a blemish on God's character.

Others think that God's wrath is inconsistent with His love. But there is no need to apologize for God's Word so long as it is fairly and graciously presented.

When we think of wrath, we get the picture of an angry schoolteacher punishing her students, or we think of an old man in heaven laughing as he throws thunderbolts down from heaven. But such images are far from the truth. The word translated wrath refers to a settled hostility that remains constant over a long period of time. Here's a working definition: God's wrath is His settled hostility to everything that contradicts His holiness. As long as God is God, He cannot overlook sin. As long as God is God, He cannot stand by indifferently while His creation is destroyed. As long as God is God, He cannot dismiss lightly those who trample His holy will. As long as God is God, He cannot wink when men mock His name.

Romans 1:18 adds a crucial fact at this point: God's wrath is revealed in response to man's rejection of the truth. The problem doesn't start with God; it starts with man. Man rejects and God responds. It's not as if He's in heaven looking for people He can send to hell. Such a view of God would be a monstrosity. But it is also true that our God will not overlook sin. He won't wink at it, laugh at it, or pretend it never happened. God's wrath is always being revealed from heaven against those who mock His name and reject His truth. That timeless truth is fulfilled in every generation.

*Eternal Father, may I never be ashamed of Your truth. Grant me courage to proclaim the whole counsel of God. Amen.*

## A MOMENT'S REFLECTION

Why is God's wrath such an unpopular doctrine today? List several ways it is often misunderstood. Why is wrath an absolutely essential part of God's character?

---
✳
---

# Nineteen

# ABOUNDING IN FAITHFULNESS: WHAT IT MEANS TO US

*But you, O Lord, are a compassionate and gracious God, slow to anger, abounding in love and faithfulness.*

Psalm 86:15

Think about the word "abounding" for a moment. To abound in money means to have all the money you need—and plenty more besides. To abound in land means your ranch is so big that it stretches beyond the horizon. To abound in faithfulness means that no one will ever reach the end of it.

This truth should give us enormous confidence in God. If you have doubted God, doubt no longer. He is faithful to keep His promises. He has ordained that someday you will be like the Lord Jesus inside and out. And He is working even now to make you a better person. Don't doubt His purposes even though you can't always see His hand at work.

God's faithfulness is the ground of our assurance. Sometimes believers struggle with assurance because we don't "feel" saved. But feelings have nothing to do with it. If you feel saved, that's good, and you should be grateful.

But if you don't feel saved, trust God to keep His word anyway. Salvation rests not on your fickle feelings but on the unchanging promises of a God who cannot lie.

If God is faithful, we have the ultimate motivation for spiritual growth. After all, if God has said He is going to sanctify you, you can rest assured that you will be sanctified—even if right now you would rather stay as you are. Your only choice is whether or not you will cooperate with God. Some of us get better slower than necessary because we fight against God's purposes. We harbor wrong attitudes—lust, bitterness, pride, sloth, envy, and all the rest—and then we wonder why it's taking us so long to get better. A little cooperation goes a long way in the area of sanctification.

Finally, God's faithfulness ought to give us perseverance in prayer. Sometimes we stop praying two days before the answer is about to come from heaven. I know many Christians who have struggled for years with certain behavior patterns and then given up simply because they were so discouraged. But the Bible tells us that God is always at work moving us toward a time when we will be perfect in every respect. Even in this life, we can make huge progress as Christians. It's just that the progress often comes slowly and in small increments. So we ought to keep on praying precisely because we believe God is at work in us even when we don't see it.

*Lord, I do not pray for more faith. I ask instead for a greater understanding of Your faithfulness. Amen.*

— ✳ —

## A MOMENT'S REFLECTION

How would you respond to a believer who says he doesn't "feel" saved? In what way is God's faithfulness the basis for our assurance? What kind of "cooperation" have you given God lately?

———— ✳ ————

# Twenty

# GOD'S FORGIVENESS: REMOVED, COVERED, AND GONE FOREVER

*Blessed is he whose transgressions are forgiven, whose sins are covered. Blessed is the man whose sin the Lord does not count against him and in whose spirit is no deceit.*

Psalm 32:1–2

P salm 32 is part of David's confession to God after his terrible sin with Bathsheba. He wrote while his hands were still red with the blood of Uriah the Hittite. At first he tried to "cover" his own sin by pretending it didn't happen. But that brought him only agony, pain, and overwhelming guilt. Eventually he came to his senses and confessed everything to God. In Romans 4:7–8 the apostle Paul quoted these verses to demonstrate what God's forgiveness means.

What happens to your sin when you trust Jesus Christ as Savior? First, it is forgiven. "Blessed are [they] whose transgressions are forgiven." The word means to "send away." It has the idea of physical removal from one location to another. When God forgives you, He removes your sins from you and takes them so far away that you will never be able to find them again.

Second, it is covered. "Whose sins are covered." The word means to "cover so completely that it can never be un-

covered again." The picture relates to the high priest's sprinkling of the blood of a sacrifice on the yearly Day of Atone-
ment. By sprinkling the blood on the mercy seat, the high
priest was acting out a picture of the bloody death of Jesus
Christ. The message is clear: The blood of Jesus is so powerful that it completely covers all your sins. All means all. If
you have trusted Christ, your sins are covered—yesterday,
today, tomorrow, and forever.

Third, it is not counted against you any longer.
"Blessed is the man whose sin the Lord does not count
against him." The verb comes from the realm of account-
ing where accounts are credited or debited. In this context, it means that once you trust Christ, your sin will
never be counted against you. God will not credit your
sin to your account. Why? Because your sin is now "credited" to Christ's account, and His righteousness is now
"credited" to your account.

Think of what is being said here. Your sins are forgiv-
en. That's total removal. Your sins are covered. That's total covering. Your sins are not counted against you. That's
total disappearance.

There is bad news and good news in the gospel. The
bad news is that you are a sinner desperately in need of
forgiveness. The good news is that through Christ all
your sins can be forgiven forever.

Christians believe in the forgiveness of sins through
the blood of Jesus Christ. Apart from Jesus, God has no
other plan and you have no other hope.

*Father, I praise You for removing my sin so completely that it can never be used against me. Thank You for Jesus, who was made sin for me that I might be made the righteousness of God in Him. Amen.*

---- ✳ ----

## A MOMENT'S REFLECTION

What evidence of sin do you see in your own life? How have you experienced God's forgiveness? Do you agree that apart from Jesus Christ, God has no other plan of salvation?

Section Three
# FIRST STEPS

*But I call to God, and the Lord saves me.*
Psalm 55:16

---
✳
---

# Twenty-One

# WHO IS JESUS?
# THE WORLD'S VERDICT—
# AND GOD'S

*All who see me mock me; they hurl insults, shaking their heads: "He trusts in the Lord; let the Lord rescue him."*

Psalm 22:7–8

In Matthew 27:43 we find these verses literally fulfilled in the death of Jesus Christ. When Jesus walked upon the face of the earth, many people thought He was a criminal. The Pharisees and the Sadducees and the temple aristocrats, the powers that be, thought He was a criminal. They thought He was a malefactor. They thought He was a rabble-rouser. They thought He was a trouble-maker. Some of them even said He was filled with demons. Do you remember that? Jesus was working miracles, and they said, "He does it by the power of the devil" (see Matthew 12:22–24).

That's really the whole story of His ministry. The common people believed in Him, but the power brokers came to the conclusion that Jesus was not a righteous man. "He's not a good man. He's a bad man. He's not a force for good. He's a force for evil. He didn't come from heaven. He really came from hell. He's not doing the work of God. He's really doing the work of Satan. He never had the power of God.

He's really filled with demons." They ultimately concluded that He was a kind of religious mad dog who had to be eliminated for the public good. In the end, they said, "This man is a bad man and we've got to get rid of Him."

So they executed Him as a criminal. And it appeared when they had executed Him that they were right. It appeared on Friday afternoon that He was nothing but a ne'er-do-well, just another in that long series of Galilean traveling prophets, just another con artist, just another charismatic rabbi who stirs up the public and then comes to no good end.

They appeared to be right for about thirty-six hours. They woke up Saturday morning and they were right. They ate lunch Saturday and they were right. They went to bed Saturday night and they were right. They woke up Sunday morning and they were wrong. Because something happened between sundown Saturday night and sunup Sunday morning.

In our political process if you're found guilty at a lower level you can appeal the case upward, and finally you will come to the Supreme Court—the court of last resort. If the case makes it to the Supreme Court, the justices have the power to overturn any guilty verdict. On Sunday morning earth's verdict was overturned and heaven spoke in favor of the Son of God. A mighty hand reached down and rolled away the stone, and the Son of God walked out from the realm of death, never to die again. When He rose from the dead, that was God's way of saying, "Not Guilty. This Man is My Son, hear Him."

*Father, thank You for proving once and for all that Jesus really is Your only begotten Son. Amen.*

—✳—

## A MOMENT'S REFLECTION

If Jesus really was the Son of God, why didn't everyone recognize that fact? Why do many people today still doubt His true identity? How did the Resurrection overturn the world's verdict?

---
✳
---

# Twenty-Two

# FORSAKEN BY GOD: WHEN JESUS PAID IT ALL

*My God, my God, why have you forsaken me?*

Psalm 22:1

Imagine that somewhere in the universe there is a cesspool containing all the sins that have ever been committed. The cesspool is deep, dark, and indescribably foul. All the evil deeds that men and women have ever done are floating there. Imagine that a river of filth constantly flows into that cesspool, replenishing the vile mixture with all the evil done every day.

Now imagine that while Jesus was on the cross, that cesspool is emptied onto Him. See the flow of filth as it settles upon Him. The flow never seems to stop. It is vile, toxic, deadly, and filled with disease, pain, and suffering.

When God looked down at His Son, He saw the cesspool of sin emptied on His head. No wonder He turned away from the sight. Who could bear to watch it?

Think of it. All the lust in the world was there. All the broken promises were there. All the murder, all the killing, all the hatred between people. Every vile deed, every wicked thought, every vain imagination—all of it was laid upon Jesus when He hung on the cross.

I take from this solemn truth two great implications:

1.  We must never minimize the horror of human sin. Sometimes we laugh and say, "The devil made me do it," as if sin were something to joke about. But it was our sin that Jesus bore that day. It was our sin that caused the Father to turn away from the Son. It was our sin floating in that cesspool of iniquity. He became a curse, and we were part of the reason. Let us never joke about sin. It is no laughing matter.

2.  We must never minimize the awful cost of our salvation. Without the Cross there would be no forgiveness. Without the Cross there would be no salvation. Without the Cross we would be lost forever. Without the Cross our sins would still be upon us. It cost Christ everything to redeem us. Let us never make light of what cost Him so dearly.

This cry from the Cross is for all the lonely people of the world. It is for the abandoned child . . . the widow . . . the divorcee struggling to make ends meet . . . the mother standing over the bed of her suffering daughter . . . the father out of work . . . the parents left alone . . . the prisoner in his cell . . . the aged persons who languish in convalescent homes . . . wives abandoned by their husbands . . . singles who celebrate their birthdays alone.

This is the word from the Cross for you. No one has ever been as alone as Jesus was. You will never be forsaken as He was. No cry of your pain can exceed the cry of His pain when God turned His back and looked the other way.

*Lord Jesus, You bore the weight of my sins that I might bear them no more. You were forsaken that I might never be alone. I cannot repay You, but I will praise You forever for so great a salvation. Amen.*

— ✳ —

## A MOMENT'S REFLECTION

How could God the Father "forsake" His Son at the Cross? What does that tell you about the cost of your salvation? Take a few moments to contemplate the Cross—and to praise God that the price for sin has been fully paid.

---

✳

---

# Twenty-Three

# JESUS:
# THE NAME YOU CAN TRUST

*The Lord is my shepherd, I shall not be in want.*

Psalm 23:1

Israel has always been a nation of shepherds. To this day one can still see shepherds herding their flocks in the hills around Bethlehem. Abraham was a shepherd, and so was David, who wrote the words of this beloved psalm. First Samuel 16 tells us that while David was tending sheep for his father Jesse he was chosen to be the king of Israel. Psalm 78:71 tells us that "from tending the sheep he [the Lord] brought him to be the shepherd of his people Jacob." David was a shepherd in one way or another all his life, and so it is not surprising that he thought of the Lord as his shepherd.

It is sometimes alleged that sheep are dumb, but that is not true. Sheep are actually smart animals who tend to lose their way without a shepherd to lead them. They go astray from the flock (Isaiah 53:6); they fall prey to vicious animals; they cannot find their way to the fold; and if someone does not come and rescue them (Luke 15:3–7), they will die in the wilderness.

Sheep need a shepherd who cares for them. A good

shepherd is everything to the sheep. He lives with them twenty-four hours a day, eats with them, sleeps with them, and leads them from pasture to quiet waters, constantly watching lest his flock be overtaken by savage wolves. The shepherd is a guide, a helper, a friend, a protector, a leader, a provider, and a healer for the wounded.

What a shepherd is for the sheep, the Lord Jesus is for His people. "I am the good shepherd. The good shepherd lays down his life for his sheep" (John 10:11). We need to ponder these words, because we live in a world where trust in leaders is at an all-time low. There was a time when public officials, business leaders, doctors, teachers, and clergy were universally trusted. If you had a title, possessed a degree, or held public office, people assumed they could trust you. Our generation has witnessed a series of shocking revelations from the White House to the courthouse to the church house that, taken together, have eroded public confidence. We live in a poisoned atmosphere where anyone in a position of authority is subject to intense skeptical scrutiny.

Yet in the midst of our doubt we still need leaders we can trust. When Jesus lists His qualifications, He simply says, "I am the good shepherd." He proved it by laying down His life for us. Here is good news for a cynical generation. If you're looking for someone to trust, take a long look at Jesus. He's the Shepherd we need.

*Loving Shepherd, help me to love You, follow You, and trust You more today than yesterday. Amen.*

——✳——

## A MOMENT'S REFLECTION

Name five qualities of a good shepherd. How does the Lord Jesus fulfill each one? Why is trust such a vital quality? What happens when leaders lose the trust of their followers?

---
✳
---

# Twenty-Four

# GUILTY AS CHARGED: THE TRUTH ABOUT THE HUMAN RACE

*All have turned aside, they have together become corrupt; there is no one who does good, not even one.*

Psalm 14:3

In South Carolina a mother shocks the world when she straps her two boys into safety seats and then plunges her car into a pond, drowning them. When questioned by the police, she denies any involvement, blaming an unknown assailant. When evidence against her mounts, she finally confesses to murdering her own flesh and blood.

A shudder runs through the national conscience. How could a mother do such a thing? Nothing is more "unnatural" than a mother intentionally harming her children. No explanation will suffice; no excuse can be accepted. This is beyond ordinary right and wrong; we are now into the realm of true moral evil.

In another part of the country a religious leader who makes veiled claims to being the Messiah leads his followers into a standoff with the government. A siege ensues that ends in a fiery conflagration. In a radio interview, one man argues that the leader must have been demon-possessed. Why? Because he did not act like a rational being. The answer must be given that sin by its very nature is not rational.

"There is no one who does good, not even one." Here is God's evaluation as He looks down from heaven. He doesn't see a single righteous person—not even one. But how can this be? How can God look down at five billion people and not see even one righteous man? Is this not an overly harsh judgment? The answer is that God judges according to a different standard than the one we use. Most of us grade on the curve. That is, we look at our neighbor and say, "Well, I'm not as bad as he is." Or we compare ourselves with someone we know at work who makes us look good by comparison.

But God doesn't judge that way. He uses the standard of His own sinless perfection. He compares us to His own perfect holiness, His own perfect love, His own perfect wisdom, His own perfect justice. And compared with God's own perfection, there is no one—not even one person—who comes close to being righteous in His eyes.

Let us make the matter more personal. There is evil in my heart and in your heart. All true religion begins with the recognition of this truth: Evil resides in every human heart. No one is exempt. Some may receive a bigger share of evil, some less, but the basic allotment is in there somewhere. If you would know God personally, you must come to grips with who you are.

You've got to take a good look at the man or the woman in the mirror. What you see, you may not like, but you must look anyway. If you don't, you'll never know who you really are. And until you know yourself, you'll never know God, for He never reveals Himself except to people who recognize their need of Him.

*Father, show me the truth about myself so that I will cling tightly to Your grace. Amen.*

— ✳ —

## A MOMENT'S REFLECTION

Do you agree that there are no "good" people on earth? How then do we explain the millions of unbelievers who apparently live moral lives and who show compassion to others? What standard will God use when He judges your life?

※

# Twenty-Five

# CONVERSION:
# NO GOD BUT GOD

*I will praise you, O Lord, with all my heart; before the "gods" I will sing your praise.*

Psalm 138:1

A few days ago a friend sent me an e-mail telling about a question posed to her by a co-worker. Here is the text of the question:

> How is a Christian defined? It used to be that if you were not Jewish or Hindu or Buddhist, you were a Christian, whether Catholic or Lutheran or Episcopal or Baptist. But it seems now that the word means something more specific. Is Christianity considered to be an actual religion other than Catholic or Lutheran or Episcopal or Baptist or whatever? If so, what makes it different?

That's a very good question. It shows that the person has been doing some serious thinking about spiritual issues. It also reveals that she has penetrated to a core issue that has long confused millions of people: What is the difference between being a Christian and being a church member?

How would you answer that question?

In one of his books Lloyd Ogilvie wrote this arresting sentence: "The great need today is for the conversion of religious people who, though they believe in God, are heading away from Him and not toward Him." He went on to say that authentic conversion always comes in response to God's call and always results in a radical reorientation of the whole life. It changes our direction, and that change stands the test of time.

Conversion begins when you turn to God. It is nothing more or less than "an intentional turning of oneself to God." Because it is intentional, it does not happen by accident. Nor does it happen automatically. Nor can anyone else turn for you. You yourself must decide to turn to God. No one can make that decision for you.

Conversion also means turning from your idols to the living and true God. When David spoke of the "gods," he meant the idols worshiped by the surrounding pagan nations. You can have your idols or you can have God, but you can't have both. The religions built upon these idols were degrading, obscene, and perverse. They generated fear, vengeance, immorality, demonism, and slavery. This idolatry was the foundation for government, religion, amusements, social clubs, and everyday labor. It permeated every aspect of society.

For a Christian to reject all that and follow Jesus Christ meant rejecting the very foundation of society itself. Yet that is what Jesus calls us to do, and until we have done it, we cannot truly claim to be converted.

*Lord Jesus, I pray to be deeply and truly and profoundly
converted in a manner so obvious that no one can doubt
that my life has truly been changed by You. Amen.*

———— ✳ ————

## A MOMENT'S REFLECTION

Name the "gods" of contemporary society. Which ones
were you following before your own conversion? Do you
agree that many religious people need to be converted?

---

✳

# Twenty-Six

# REPENTANCE:
# A DECISIVE TURNING
# TO GOD

*All the ends of the earth will remember and turn to the Lord,
and all the families of the nations will bow down before
him.*

Psalm 22:27

Charles Spurgeon comments that this verse displays
"Messiah's missionary spirit." Christ intends that all
the nations turn from their sin and worship Him. Spurgeon adds that in this verse we have the proper order of
conversion: remembering, turning, and worshiping.

At the heart of it all is "turning" to the Lord. The
Bible sometimes uses the term "repentance" to describe
this act. In the Old Testament there are two primary Hebrew words for repentance. The first word means to turn
around or to change the mind. The second word is used
more than six hundred times in the Old Testament and is
translated by such words as "turn," "return," "seek," "restore." The word occurs often in phrases like "to turn to
the Lord with all your heart."

The primary New Testament word for repentance
means "to change the mind." When you repent, you are
changing your mind in a fundamental way. It has to do

with the way you think about something. You've been thinking one way, but now you think the opposite way. That's repentance—the changing of the mind.

A true changing of the mind about any important issue will always change the way you think about it, talk about it, feel about it, and act about it. I'm suggesting that true repentance is more than just a little game you play in your mind. Repentance is a decisive change in direction. It's a change of mind, which leads to a change of thinking, which leads to a change of attitude, which leads to a change of feeling, which leads to a change of values, which leads to a change in the way you lead your life.

I can remember thirty years ago going to a small Baptist church out in the country to hear Ed McCollum—my father in the ministry—preach in a revival meeting. It was one of those little white church buildings where farmers go to church on Sunday. I've never forgotten how Pastor McCollum explained the doctrine of repentance. He went to one end of the platform and started walking, and about the time he got to the other end, he turned around and started going in the other direction. He said, "That's what repentance is. You were going one way in your life, and now you are going in another." That's why the typical Old Testament word for repentance is "turn." Turning is always involved in repentance. It's a change of mind that leads to a change of direction.

*Father, without You I never would have turned at all.
Through Your Spirit I was given the gift of repentance
that I might turn from idols to serve the living and true
God. Thank You. Amen.*

—— ✳ ——

## A MOMENT'S REFLECTION

If repentance means to "change the mind," what kinds of
things does an unbeliever need to change his mind about
before he can be saved? Why is repentance fundamental
to true conversion? Why must repentance always lead to
a changed life?

※

# Twenty-Seven

# TRUSTING JESUS: YOUR ONLY HOPE OF SALVATION

*But as for me, I trust in you.*

Psalm 55:23

It happened early in the week. A friend said, "Preach well this Sunday. Someone I love will be in the service. I want my friend to know Jesus." What a wonderful encouragement to a pastor's heart.

All week long I was thinking about how to end my sermon. The answer came while I was driving home from a hospital visit. I happened to catch a few minutes of an interview with Pastor Erwin Lutzer as he discussed God's plan of salvation. I listened as a woman called with a gripping question. She said that all her friends would be surprised if they heard her call, because they all looked to her as a good Christian. But in her heart she had no assurance. She prayed the sinner's prayer every day just to be sure. Her question was simple: "How can I be sure I'm going to heaven?"

Pastor Lutzer gave a wonderful answer. "I want you to think about the cross of Christ and what it represents. Do you believe that what Jesus did on the cross was enough for your salvation? Or do you think you need to add anything to what Jesus did?"

That's really the central question for all of us to consider. When Jesus died, was His death enough so that there is nothing else you need to do for your own salvation? If the answer is yes, then you can be saved and you can also be sure. If the answer is no, then you can never be sure because you can never do enough.

Thank God the answer is an eternal yes. "Jesus paid it all, All to Him I owe; Sin had left a crimson stain, He washed it white as snow." Can you make the following statements?

- "I believe the Cross was enough for me."
- "I am willing to trust Jesus Christ completely and absolutely!"
- "I want to go to heaven, and I'm trusting Jesus to take me there."
- "I'm trusting my whole life into Jesus' almighty hands."

If you want to be saved, run to the cross of Christ. Lay hold of Jesus by faith. Fix all your hope on Him. Those who trust in Jesus will never be disappointed.

Do you know Jesus? Have you ever met Him personally? His name is the greatest name in all the universe. It doesn't matter who else you know or don't know. You may know leaders and kings and presidents and potentates, but if you don't know Jesus, you've missed the reason for your own existence.

Do you know Him?

*Lord Jesus, nothing is more important than knowing You. I pray for deep assurance that I have trusted You as my Savior. Amen.*

———— ✳ ————

A MOMENT'S REFLECTION

"Do you know Him?" If this is the most important question, you need to think about it. What is your answer? If you aren't sure, take a moment to pray along the lines suggested in this entry.

---
✳
---

# Twenty-Eight

# SOVEREIGN GRACE: HOW A SLAVE TRADER MET JESUS

*He reached down from on high and took hold of me; he drew me out of deep waters.*

Psalm 18:16

Either you are converted or you aren't. You have turned or you haven't. Unless you are converted you will never go to heaven.

How can you be converted? The answer is simple. You must transfer your trust away from yourself and place it fully upon Jesus Christ. You must turn from self-worship, good works, and every idol in your life and wholly depend upon Jesus Christ and Him alone as your Lord and Savior.

The Christian life begins with conversion! Without conversion there is no Christian life. And if you are not converted, you are not a Christian at all.

John Newton was born in 1725, the son of an English sea captain. At the age of eleven he went to sea for the first time. Forced to join the Royal Navy, he tried to escape but was arrested in West Africa. He became the slave of a white slave trader's black wife. For two years he lived in hunger and destitution.

He eventually became a slave-ship captain, taking black Africans to the Mediterranean and the West Indies. In 1747 he boarded a ship for England, but a violent storm in the North Atlantic hit the ship, which began to fill with water. The timbers broke away from the side. An ordinary ship would have gone to the bottom immediately, but they were carrying a load of beeswax and wool that was lighter than water.

In the midst of the struggle to save the ship, the young man said to himself almost without thinking, "If this will not do, the Lord have mercy on us." By his own word, it was the first desire for mercy he had felt in many years. That was the turning point of his life.

He left the slave trade and later entered the ministry in Olney, England. He soon became known as a great preacher who attracted enormous crowds. He wrote nearly three hundred hymns—most of which have long since been forgotten. But some we still sing—"Glorious Things of Thee Are Spoken," "How Sweet the Name of Jesus Sounds," and the one hymn that is perhaps the most famous hymn of all time. Around the world Christians sing it in dozens of languages:

> Amazing grace! how sweet the sound
> That saved a wretch like me!
> I once was lost, but now am found,
> Was blind, but now I see.

Before he died, he prepared his own epitaph, which reads:

John Newton, once an infidel and libertine, a servant of slaves in Africa, was, by the rich mercy of our Lord and Savior Jesus Christ, preserved, restored, pardoned, and appointed to preach the faith he had long labored to destroy.

That's what God can do. That's true conversion.

*Holy Father, I bless You for the mighty miracle of conversion. I pray to be used by You in the conversion of many sinners to Jesus Christ. Amen.*

——— ✳ ———

## A MOMENT'S REFLECTION

Are you converted? What is your testimony of God's grace in your life? Take a moment and rehearse your own story. Now pray that God will give you a chance to tell it to someone this week.

---

✳

# Twenty-Nine

# SAINTS:
# GOD'S HOLY ONES

*For the Lord takes delight in his people; he crowns the humble with salvation. Let the saints rejoice in this honor and sing for joy on their beds.*

Psalm 149:4–5

The Bible uses a particular word that is often applied to Christians. We use this word today but not necessarily in the same way. What we mean when we use the word and what the biblical writers meant when they used the word is generally not the same thing. Because of the confusion, many Christians hesitate to use this word to describe themselves.

I refer to the great biblical word *saint*. Instantly you see what I mean. It's not a word that readily comes to mind. To us "saint" has a particular meaning. It refers to a great Christian, long dead, whose life was marked by unusual piety. Thus we speak of Saint Paul, Saint James, Saint Christopher, Saint Jude, Saint Nicholas, and Saint Eligius. The whole point of that sense of the word is that they are saints and we are not. In theory at least, they have achieved a rank far beyond anything we weary pilgrims can ever hope to achieve.

The truth of the matter is quite different. The Bible never uses the word saint to refer to a select group of super-

Christians. Rather, it was routinely applied in the New Testament to every Christian. This means that every Christian is a saint of God. To put it another way, if you aren't a saint from the Bible's point of view, you're not a Christian at all.

This means it is perfectly legitimate to refer to your fellow Christians as saints. We have no problem calling each other "brother" and "sister." There is at least as much biblical precedent to speak of "Saint Karen," "Saint Henry," "Saint Greg," "Saint Mike," and so on.

We know the word Christian means "a follower of Christ," disciple means "a learner," and a believer is "one who believes in Jesus." What does the word saint mean? Stripped of everything else, it means "holy one." The New Testament saints were "the holy ones."

What is a saint, then? A saint is a person who is holy. In some ways that seems as odd a description. Most of us probably don't feel very holy. And most of us struggle with unholy thoughts and attitudes more than we would like to admit. But the Bible tells a different story. We who struggle so much with sin are called saints by God. Let that thought lift your spirits the next time you feel like a failure. If you feel unworthy of sainthood, remember that God does the choosing, and He does it on the basis of grace, not human merit. Rejoice in the honor of being called a saint of God. When you go to bed tonight, sing for joy. It's amazing how far God will go to show us how much He loves us.

*Lord God, thank You for numbering me among Your saints—even when I am very aware of being a sinner. Amen.*

## A MOMENT'S REFLECTION

What do you think of when you hear the word *saint*? How would you feel if someone called you a saint? Complete this sentance: "My name is Saint _____" Which parts of your life seem least "saintly" right now?

---

*✳*

---

# Thirty

# HARD HEARTS: WHY YOU CAN'T ARGUE PEOPLE INTO GOD'S KINGDOM

*In spite of all this, they kept on sinning; in spite of his wonders, they did not believe.*

Psalm 78:32

Have you ever been witnessing to a friend, trying to convince him of his need for salvation, and you talked until you were blue in the face and got nowhere? You pulled out Josh McDowell and you read from *Evidence That Demands a Verdict*. You got out the "Four Spiritual Laws" and you read it. You started at Law One and went to Law Four and then started at Law Four and went back to Law One. Then you quoted Billy Graham and you quoted John Calvin. Then you quoted Martin Luther and the gospel of John and you gave your own testimony. You told your friend everything you knew. And by the time you were finished the person was just as hardened to the gospel as he was at the beginning.

That very thing has happened to me more than once. Sometimes I run into people who will not believe no matter what I say to them. It's almost like there's a barrier between me and them. As a matter of fact, there is a barrier between me and them, which is why it is impossible to argue anybody into the kingdom of God. You cannot do it. You cannot by human reason just throw the book at someone and talk him into being a Christian. It doesn't work that way. Conviction of sin is the work of the Holy Spirit. Unless the Holy Spirit is working through you and in the heart of that person, he will listen and just brush it off and go on as if you hadn't said anything to him at all.

Some people don't believe because they don't want to believe—and nothing you can say can convince them otherwise. Sometimes we wonder why unbelievers won't respond to our arguments. Even after we answer all their questions and fully explain the gospel, why won't they come to Christ? It's because their questions weren't the real problem. The questions were a smoke screen to cover up a hardened heart.

Only the Holy Spirit can convict men and women of their sin before God (John 16:8–11). That isn't easy to do. It's easy to get people to admit they're not perfect. Almost everybody will admit that. It's easy to get people to admit that they have done things wrong from time to time. It's easy to get people to admit they have made mistakes. But it is difficult to get men and women to admit they are sinners before a holy, righteous, and just God. In fact, it is so difficult it is humanly impossible.

That's why you can't argue a person into the kingdom. The next time you tell others about Christ, be bold, be gracious, and keep smiling. Let the Holy Spirit do the rest.

*Spirit of God, give me holy boldness and a winsome spirit as I talk about Christ with others. Amen.*

— ✳ —

## A MOMENT'S REFLECTION

Have you ever had an experience similar to the one described above? How can we convince sinners of their need for a Savior? What usually happens when we try to argue people into God's kingdom?

# THE SCHOOL OF SUFFERING

*It was good for me to be afflicted so that I might learn your decrees.*

Psalm 119:71

---

※

---

# Thirty-One

# AFFLICTION:
# A TEST OF OUR MOTIVES

*But he lifted the needy out of their affliction and increased their families like flocks.*

Psalm 107:41

A recent popular song declares, "Life is hard but God is good." There is a world of truth in those seven words. Life is hard—not just for some of us but for all of us eventually. Sickness comes, heartache comes, old age comes, and death comes. Although heaven itself is a free gift, the road to the celestial city is paved with "many dangers, toils, and snares." Thankfully, in the midst of our trials—and sometimes because of our trials—we discover that God is good in every circumstance of life.

God often sends trouble following a period of prosperity in order that He may test our motives. Are we serving Him just because things are going well? What if we lose our job? Our marriage? Our friends? Our reputation? Our wealth? Our home? Our health? Will we still serve Him then? That, by the way, is the question that Satan posed to God regarding His servant Job: "Does Job fear God for nothing?" (Job 1:9). He then accuses God of having rigged the game by putting a hedge of comfort and blessing around Job. "Sure, You've blessed him. No wonder he serves You. Who wouldn't? But take everything away and he will curse You to Your face." Everything that happened to Job was sent as a test to prove whether or not Satan was right.

So why are you serving God? Is it only because things are going well for you? When life tumbles in, what then?

Recently I spoke with a man in our church who has been diagnosed with cancer. The doctors told him that his cancer is both inoperable and incurable. What do you do then? When I spoke with this godly man he said something like this, "God has been so good to me. He's never let me down for all these years. No matter what happens, I win. If I'm cured, I get to enjoy life for a few more years. If I die, I go to heaven." A few days ago he told someone else that he had no complaints because after all God has done for him, why should he complain about cancer?

I don't know what the future holds for my friend, but I know that he has already passed the test. His motives are pure because his heart is fixed on the Lord, not on his circumstances. Let us all take the lesson to heart. Fix your eyes on Jesus, and when the waters rise, you will still be safe.

*Lord Jesus, help me to see You in the midst of my trials and to trust when I cannot see. Amen.*

— ✳ —

## A MOMENT'S REFLECTION

In what ways has life been hard on you? What evidence do you see of God's goodness? Are you willing to serve God even when your circumstances aren't the best?

*Thirty-Two*

---- ✳ ----

# THE BENEFITS OF PAIN: SEEING GOD IN A CRISIS

*Then they cried to the Lord in their trouble, and he saved them from their distress.*

Psalm 107:19

It happened during a trip to the area where I grew up. My youngest son and I journeyed back home in order to surprise my mother on her seventy-fifth birthday. It was the first time that my brothers and I had gotten together in seven years. We truly did surprise her, and that was worth the entire trip.

While I was in town, someone I did not know asked to meet with me. I agreed, and I ended up spending about an hour talking with a woman whose marriage was on the verge of total collapse.

The names were new, but the story was old. After twenty years of marriage, her husband was bored and frustrated. So he moved out to live by himself. She wanted to make the marriage work, but more than that, she wanted to know God better. Could I help her?

She put it this way. "For twenty years my husband has been the center of my life. Now that he's left, I've discovered that I can't build my life around him. For the first time, I've learned that Jesus Christ must be the center of my life."

When we finished talking I told her two things. "First, I can't guarantee that your husband will come back. He might or he might not, and there's nothing you can do to guarantee that your marriage will survive. Second, you're going to be all right as long as you keep seeking the Lord. You've been asking God to show Himself to you in a new way. That's a prayer God will always answer."

As I thought about it later, it occurred to me that God often reveals Himself to us in a crisis situation. Not long after that trip I spoke with a woman whose godly husband died at a relatively young age, leaving her with several children to raise. Through her tears she spoke of how much she has learned about God in the weeks since her husband's death. She would not ask to have him back in exchange for the things God has taught her about Himself. So it is that we learn more in the shadows than in the sunlight.

None of us would choose to go through a crisis in order to learn more about God. We rarely have a choice. But we do have a choice about whether we will learn from a crisis and use it as an opportunity to grow closer to God. Hard times come to all of us sooner or later. If our hearts are open, through our tears we can learn more about our heavenly Father than we ever knew before.

*Almighty God, help me to respond graciously to the unexpected things that will happen to me today. Amen.*

114

---— ✳ —---

## A MOMENT'S REFLECTION

How much is knowing God worth to you? Who or what is the center of your life right now? Take a moment to thank God for revealing Himself to you through the hard times of life.

---
✳
---

# Thirty-Three

# A PERSONAL QUESTION: IS GOD ENOUGH FOR YOU?

*My flesh and my heart may fail, but God is the strength of my heart and my portion forever.*

Psalm 73:26

Here are two stories from the same day. She is an educator with a Ph.D., and he is a distinguished lawyer. Although they were quite successful in their respective careers, something was missing. That something was a personal relationship with Jesus Christ. When they met Him, He transformed their lives to the point that they felt called to do something to help the poor in their native land. A few years ago they moved to Southern California, where they direct a ministry of compassion aimed at the Philippines. Now they spend more than half their time in the Philippines in mission work among the poor. As we talked I was impressed by the fact that even though they could have stayed in America and lived at the top of the ladder, they have chosen to sacrifice for those at the bottom.

I met the husband and wife at 9 A.M. on Friday. At noon I ate lunch with a man who also enjoyed the best that life had to offer. By the time he was twenty-two or twenty-three, he was on the fast track to success. At one point he was the youngest CFO of any major company in America. He had it all—the money, the cars, the big home, the nice clothes, all the outward marks of success.

A few years later he came to Jesus Christ. Inwardly his life began to change, but outwardly he devoted himself to money and success. Four years later as he sat in church, he felt God calling him to leave his profession and serve the Lord full time. Even though he knew what God wanted, for seven years he fought the call, all the while making more and more money and fighting a battle within his own heart. Three years ago God literally knocked him flat on his face as he took a shower one morning. That was the turning point of his life. A year later when he resigned his position, the news made the front pages of the local paper. Soon he and his wife and their two daughters left to start a coffeehouse ministry in Ireland. Why would a man uproot his family like that? Because God has called him to spread the life-changing gospel of Jesus Christ. He is going by faith, putting aside a promising career to obey the call of God. He has no doubts, no worries, and no regrets.

As I think about the couple living in the Philippines and the family going to Ireland, I am impressed by their joy. Don't talk to them about sacrifice. Don't pity them for setting aside their careers. God's call is their career, and if it happens to take them overseas, then so be it. If it brings them back to the States later, then so be it. They have discovered what it means to say that God is their "portion forever."

Is God enough for you? Or do you also need what the world has to offer?

*O Lord, bring me to the place where nothing the world offers can satisfy me as much as knowing You. Amen.*

—— ✳ ——

A MOMENT'S REFLECTION

Ponder the last two questions of this entry. How would you answer them? In what sense is God your "portion forever"?

# Thirty-Four

# TRUSTING GOD:
# A CHOICE—NOT A FEELING

*In God, whose word I praise, in God I trust; I will not be afraid. What can mortal man do to me?*

Psalm 56:4

Can you trust God? Or better, Can God be trusted? More and more I am convinced that this is the fundamental question of life: "Is God good, and can He be trusted to do what is right?" If the answer is yes, then we can face the worst that life has to offer. If the answer is no, then we're no better off than the people who have no faith at all. In fact, if the answer is no or if we're not sure, then we really don't have any faith anyway.

While doing a radio interview for a station in Yakima, Washington, I was asked how I could be so positive and confident when I spoke about God's will. The man asking the question seemed burdened with many cares and difficulties. My answer went this way: "Twenty-two years ago when my father died, I came face-to-face with the ultimate unanswerable question of life. I didn't know then why such a good man would have to die at the age of fifty-six, or why He would leave my mother and her four sons without a husband and a father. I had no clue about what God was doing. In the years since then I have learned many things about life, but I confess that I still don't understand why my father died. It doesn't make any more sense to me now than it did then.

"I am older and wiser, but in the one question that really matters I have no answers. I have learned since then that faith is a choice you make. Sometimes you choose to believe because of what you see; often you believe in spite of what you can see. As I look to the world around me, many things remain mysterious and unanswerable. But if there is no God, or if He is not good, then nothing at all makes sense. I have chosen to believe because I must believe. I truly have no other choice. If I sound confident, it is only because I have learned through my tears that my only confidence is in God and God alone."

My older brother is a urologist who recently lost a twenty-year-old patient to a rare form of kidney cancer. When he asked me in all seriousness, "Why did he die?" I had no answer. But I felt no shame in saying that. I believe that God is good and can be trusted no matter what happens. If I didn't believe that, I wouldn't have the strength to get out of bed every day.

*Eternal God, You alone give meaning and purpose to life. Apart from You, nothing in this world makes sense. Amen.*

— ✳ —

## A MOMENT'S REFLECTION

Do you believe God can be trusted? Why or why not? What gives you the strength to go on when faced with unexplainable tragedy?

*

# Thirty-Five

# THE UNSEEN GOD: WHY GOD HIDES HIS FACE

*Do not hide your face from your servant; answer me quickly, for I am in trouble.*

Psalm 69:17

This verse raises an interesting question. Why would God hide His face from His servant? Why would He seem to disappear in the moment of trouble? Surely the Lord knows how much we need Him. The answer can be found along these lines: Often God seems to leave us alone for the very purpose of bringing us to the end of our human resources. As long as we think we can finagle our way out of a crisis, it's easy to think that we don't really need God at all. It is like the woman who, when told by the doctor that she should pray, replied, "My soul, is it that bad?" In truth, without God it is always "that bad"; it's just that we don't realize it until the bottom caves in.

There is a second reason God hides Himself. He does it so that He might be seen only by those with eyes of faith. The word "hide" can also be translated "veil." In ancient times kings would put veils before their chambers so that only those who truly knew the king would find the entrance. Sometimes God's face is veiled from our sight so that we might exercise our faith in the darkness.

Jesus said a similar thing when asked why He taught so much in parables. Those simple stories were given so that unbelievers would be baffled but His followers would understand. In a similar vein, the New Testament seems to indicate that after His resurrection Jesus was seen only by believers. Why? Because unbelievers wouldn't appreciate the fact that He had been raised from the dead.

The third reason brings us to the point of the text. God often hides Himself so that He might test our motives. Are we praying simply to get out of trouble, or because we want to glorify God in all that we do? Do we desire an answer to our prayers, or will we be content if the Lord Himself is the answer?

God has ordered the moral universe so that His purposes are advanced as much through suffering as they are through prosperity. This does not make suffering easy, but it does give us a new—and higher—perspective. Should we, like David, pray for God to answer us speedily in the moment of crisis? Yes, of course, and let us then wait for God to answer—in His own time, in His own way, according to His own will.

*Father, thank You for being there even when I think You are not there. Amen.*

---*---

## A MOMENT'S REFLECTION

How do you respond when God answers No to your prayers? Can you remember a time when God answered Yes—but in a way completely unexpected? What does that teach you about God?

*Thirty-Six*

---

✳

# DELIVERANCE: GOD'S PROMISE TO HIS CHILDREN

*A thousand may fall at your side, ten thousand at your right hand, but it will not come near you.*

Psalm 91:7

This verse has sustained many a believer in the heat of battle. How is it that a general can lead his troops into the teeth of withering enemy fire? Is it not because he believes so fervently in his cause that he considers himself invincible to enemy bullets? By the same token, this verse encourages us to believe that when we face opposition on every side, we can enter the fray knowing that nothing can harm us unless God wills it. Sometimes we are spared altogether, sometimes we are wounded that we might trust even more in our God, and sometimes we are hit but are not hurt at all.

Thus, this verse teaches us that we may have extraordinary courage in the moment of great crisis. We can stand when others fall around us. We can face our problems boldly. We can go into surgery with confidence, we can be dragged into court, we can be called on the carpet at work, we can face dangers as we travel. We can do all that because we know the Lord is with us.

Does this mean nothing bad can happen to the child of God? No, because bad things happen to God's people all the time. Romans 8:28 tells us that "all things work together for good to them that love God"(KJV), yet just a few verses later Paul spoke of peril, nakedness, the sword, persecution and famine (vv. 35–36). All these things—and more—happen to Christians.

What affirmatively is Psalm 91 telling us?

1. God's care extends to the tiniest details of life.
2. Nothing bad happens to us by chance.
3. God is able to deliver us in the worst circumstances.

Nothing can touch the child of God that has not first passed through His hands of love. Does that include the worst? Yes, it does. Nothing can hurt us without God's permission. Nothing. Not the enemy. Not financial ruin. Not divorce. Not lies and slander. Not cancer. Not strange accidents. Not the slings and arrows of outrageous fortune. Not gossip. Not disrespectful children. Not an unfaithful husband. Not a sudden loss of a job. Not scandal, rumor, and innuendo. Not an unfair lawsuit. Not a failed insurance policy. Not even death itself. Not Satan and his tricks. Not the fiery darts of the devil. Not the demons of hell. None of it can touch us except by God's permission.

Most of the time we won't understand when arrows do hit us. But in our confusion, our despair, our uncertainty, when we don't know anything else, this much we do know:

God has planned it all for our good and His glory. For the children of God, there are no accidents. Only incidents.

The hymn writer said it well, "When all around my soul gives way, He then is all my hope and stay. On Christ, the solid Rock, I stand; All other ground is sinking sand; All other ground is sinking sand."

*Lord, You are the solid rock of my life. Give me firm footing so that I will not slide off. Amen.*

— ✳ —

## A MOMENT'S REFLECTION

Do you agree that nothing bad can happen to you without God's permission? How does that truth affect the way you view your problems? Name an "accident" that became an "incident" that God used in a positive way in your life.

# Thirty-Seven

# HELP!
# A ONE-WORD PRAYER

*He will call upon me, and I will answer him; I will be with him in trouble, I will deliver him and honor him.*

Psalm 91:15

What is the simplest prayer of all? Help! When you don't know what else to pray, that will usually do just fine.

Psalm 91:14–16 shows us God's eight-fold deliverance of His people:

1. I will rescue him.
2. I will protect him.
3. I will answer him.
4. I will be with him.
5. I will deliver him.
6. I will honor him.
7. I will satisfy him.
8. I will save him.

There is a progression here. First, God meets us where we are. He finds us in the moment of our deep need. Second, He promises to be with us no matter what we are going through. Third, He will deliver us—sooner or later, one way or the other. Fourth, He promises to bestow glory and honor upon us. Fifth, He satisfies us with a full life—not long years necessarily, but fullness of life no matter how many years we mark on the calendar. Sixth, He will one day show us the full extent of His salvation when we see Jesus in heaven.

Thus, God draws a line from the difficulties of this life and says, "Follow Me and I will lead you straight to heaven." We think our problems are so large. God says, "Don't sweat the small stuff. I'm going to take you to heaven someday. I can handle your problems."

This week I read about a woman who said, "Before I go to bed, I give all my problems to the Lord. He's going to be up all night anyway." Indeed He is.

Not long ago I began taking inventory of my problems—and felt greatly discouraged. All of them are bigger than I am. Every one is beyond my puny strength to solve by myself.

As I pondered the matter, one insight seemed to help: God has promised to be with me. He has invited me to call upon Him for all my needs. He has said He would be with me in the time of trouble and would at the right moment deliver me. Even Satan himself cannot harm me without God's divine permission. With that confidence, I go on.

I like the way Eugene Peterson translated verse 14: "'If you'll hold on to me for dear life,' says God, 'I'll get you out of any trouble'" (The Message). You don't have to deliver yourself. You don't even have to try. All you have to do is hold on for dear life. God Himself will do the rest.

Whatever your problem, whatever your difficulty, whatever things keep you awake at night, hold on for dear life. Help is on the way.

*Father, I rest in the confidence that I will be delivered from all my difficulties sooner or later. Grant that it might be sooner. Amen.*

— ✳ —

## A MOMENT'S REFLECTION

Take an inventory of your problems, worries, and current concerns. Which ones does it seem you can handle? Which ones obviously need divine intervention? Spend some time committing each one to the Lord.

---
✳
---

# Thirty-Eight

# RIGHTEOUS ANGER: KEEP COOL AND KEEP QUIET

*In your anger do not sin; when you are on your beds, search your hearts and be silent.*

Psalm 4:4

P aul quoted the first part of this verse in Ephesians 4:26, where he added this application: "Do not let the sun go down while you are still angry." The principle is easy to grasp: Solving problems now saves trouble later. And delayed reconciliation means increased animosity. Not all anger is sinful, but anger is such a powerful emotion that when we fail to deal with it properly, it can easily harden into malice, rage, or even murder (see Matthew 5:21–26). Dealing with anger in a righteous fashion is more important than going to church; it's more important than giving money; it's more important than praying in public or going to a Bible study.

Jesus taught us that uncontrolled anger is really a form of murder in the heart. But you say, "I'm no murderer." That's what you are if you harbor bitterness and resentment in your heart toward someone else. A murderer in church? How could that be? Because anger fills your heart, because you are prone to abusive speech, because you harbor resentment toward others. Some Christians I know are so cruel in their speech that they leave a trail of bloody words wherever they go.

God's message is clear: Either you learn to control your anger, or your anger will destroy you from the inside out. Let me ask three questions that probe at a deep level:

1. Do you find it easy to lose your temper when things don't go your way?
2. Are you carrying a chip on your shoulder?
3. Is your anger keeping you from reconciling with those who have hurt you?

We need a spiritual alarm within that would begin to sound the moment anger takes over. "Ring! Ring! Ring! Danger! Murder Ahead!"

Where anger prevails, murder cannot be far behind. Given the right circumstances all of us would commit murder. Our hands are not clean because our lips are not clean.

Why bring this up? Because we are guilty of the very thing we said we would never do. We Christians tend to be very quick to excuse ourselves. Please understand that the Lord Jesus is not as quick as we are to let us off the hook. If we take Him seriously, then we've got to stop making excuses for our hidden anger, our buried resentments, and our tongue that is as sharp as a razor.

Don't bury your anger. Deal with it. Talk it out with a friend. Take it to the Lord in prayer. Don't go to bed angry or you'll wake up with a short fuse.

*Lord Jesus, when I am angry, teach me to forgive as You forgave those who sinned against You. Amen.*

———✳———

## A MOMENT'S REFLECTION

Consider the three questions in this entry. Which ones are true of you right now? What are you going to do about it?

---
✳
---

# Thirty-Nine

# ENDURANCE: TAKING THE LONG VIEW OF LIFE

*For his anger lasts only a moment, but his favor lasts a life-time; weeping may remain for a night, but rejoicing comes in the morning.*

Psalm 30:5

The following message comes from a young man in a state penitentiary:

> Prison has been a place to grow spiritually. Everything Satan does against me God can and will use to His glory. "For we know that all things work together for good to them that love God who are called according to his purpose." Romans 8:28

> A few days ago I got a letter from the Parole Board. They put off my parole for at least two more years. Please don't feel sorry for me. Rejoice with me. Remember God created the earth in six days. Just imagine what he can do in my life in two more years.

I'm going to take his advice and not feel sorry for him. As bad as it is to be in prison, it's good to be there if it brings you back to God. And it's better to be in prison in the will of God than to be on the streets and far from Him. There are many kinds of freedom in the world and many kinds of bondage. Though my friend is not a free man legally, he is freer today than many people I know.

After I told this story to my congregation, a young, well-dressed man came up to speak with me. Speaking with deep emotion he said, "Pastor, you don't know this, but I've spent time in prison. I've been exactly where that man is today. And what you said is true. It doesn't matter what got you there; it only matters how you respond."

Although I wish it were not so, I know that many people who read these words are going through hard times right now. As I have thought about the matter, I have concluded that even if I had the power (which I don't), I wouldn't take the pain away or make the hard times disappear. God has ordained that your trials are part of His plan to make you like Jesus. There are no shortcuts to spiritual maturity. Were I to take away the pain, I might move too soon and block God's work in your life. Because I see things from a human perspective, I might actually hurt you instead of help you, even though my motives would be good.

It is not "good" to suffer, but suffering is good if it leads us back to the Lord. The Bible tells us that weeping may endure for a night, but joy comes in the morning. Let us therefore endure our trials with grace and even with joy, knowing that in the end the clouds will part and the sun will shine again.

*When I feel like giving up on life, Lord, grant me the gift of endurance so I won't give up on You. Amen.*

— ✳ —

## A MOMENT'S REFLECTION

In what areas of life do you need endurance right now? Can you think of times when God used pain to promote spiritual growth? What happens when we try to take a "shortcut" in order to get out of a difficult situation?

---
*

# Forty

# GOD'S MIRACLE FORMULA: IMPOSSIBLE, DIFFICULT, DONE

*He divided the sea and led them through; he made the water stand firm like a wall.*

Psalm 78:13

J. Hudson Taylor, pioneer missionary to China, said these words: "There are three stages in any great work attempted for God: impossible, difficult, done." When God wants to do something big, He starts with something very small. When He wants to do the miraculous, He starts with the impossible. After all, when He sent His Son to the world, He didn't send Him to New York or Chicago or even to Rome. He sent Him to a little village called Bethlehem. God loves to start small, because then He can show His power in a mighty way. He also is the only One who gets the credit, because most of us don't want the credit for small beginnings. We'd rather start big and go from there. And we expect things to move rather quickly.

It's not hard to see why we think that way. After all, when we do something for the Lord, our motives are lifted to a higher plane. We pray for God's guidance, we search the Scriptures for guidance, and we believe that God is honored with our efforts.

And still things move slowly. What we hope to finish in days takes months. Soon a year passes, and then another year, and it seems as if our wheels are stuck in mud. Faith lags, enthusiasm wanes, the curious become skeptical, and nagging, ragged doubts take dead aim at our confidence. One thing we quickly learn: It won't be as easy as we thought. And the fact that we are doing it for the Lord seems to make no difference at all.

Why should it be so? Couldn't the Lord set this up another way? The answer, of course, is that He could—and sometimes He does. But mostly God lets us struggle and sweat and continue to trust in Him.

In the end we come at last to the Red Sea. The Egyptian army is moving in from the rear. To the left and right is the desert. And up ahead the impassable sea. This is life for all of us. The bad news is that there is no natural way through the Red Sea. The good news is that God loves to start with impossibility.

Whenever we start out to do something great or important or truly worthwhile, in the beginning it always seems impossible. And the more worthwhile it is, the more impossible it will seem. Cheer up! When we work for God, what starts out impossible soon becomes difficult and eventually is done.

*Loving Lord, my life seems filled with impossibilities. Give me the courage to step forward by faith, trusting You for the miracles I need. Amen.*

——— ✳ ———

## A MOMENT'S REFLECTION

Name several biblical examples where God used something small (or something very unlikely) to accomplish something great. If you could ask God to do one thing for you that seems impossible right now, what would it be? Where have you seen the "impossible, difficult, done" cycle in your own experience?

Section Five
# HARD WORDS

*The arrogant cannot stand in your presence; you hate all who do wrong.*

Psalm 5:5

---
✳
---

# Forty-One

# SPIRITUAL WARFARE: A CALL TO ARMS

*For you have been my refuge, a strong tower against the foe.*
Psalm 61:3

We are to cast our cares on the Lord, but we are not to be careless. Indeed, the opposite is true. We are, instead, to keep watch for the Enemy. We live in a fallen world where Satan is the "ruler of the kingdom of the air" (Ephesians 2:2). First John 5:19 tells us that "the whole world is under the control of the evil one." It is no wonder then that Satan goes about as a roaring lion seeking those he can destroy (1 Peter 5:8). Have you ever seen a roaring lion at the zoo? Even behind bars and a moat, a roaring lion is a fearful thing. Satan is like that. He's crafty, cruel, restless, vicious, brutal, ever threatening. That Christian is a fool who believes himself immune to Satan's attacks. The Jerusalem Bible says that Satan walks about like a roaring lion "looking for someone to eat." Get it straight. Satan is hungry, and gullible Christian is on the menu.

Satan's method is constantly to seek out our weak points. That's why he prowls about. How foolish to say we will never fall. Every one of us has a weak point, and most of us have more than one. It may be an area of temptation; it may be a bad habit; it may be a besetting sin. Or our weakness may be disguised as an area we think is our strength, such as our speech or our looks or our education or our personality. Just think of this: If you know your strengths and weaknesses, the devil does too. And he knows just how to attack.

Our consolation is that many other believers are under satanic attack and they are standing firm. It's not as if we're the only ones having it rough. Consider your brothers and sisters in distant lands facing persecution for Christ every day. Let their example help keep you strong.

Our only hope is constant vigilance against the Enemy. Oliver Cromwell told his troops, "Trust in God and keep your powder dry." Resist the devil. Stand like a granite wall against his infernal attacks. The attack may come at any moment. And he may attack from any direction. Expose a weakness, and there the devil will come in.

Remember, it is his job to sow discord among the brethren. Whenever you see a church torn apart with controversy, rest assured old Screwtape's boss has done his work well. If left unchecked, he will destroy an entire church.

You are not immune to Satan's schemes. The moment you feel invincible, you have played right into his hands. So, resist him and let your faith be a solid wall.

*Lord of Hosts, You have given me everything I need to be victorious in the day of battle. May I not foolishly rely on my own strength but wholly rest on You alone. Amen.*

—— ✳ ——

## A MOMENT'S REFLECTION

Name the "tools" Satan uses to tempt you to sin. What are your weak points? What steps can you take today to resist the devil?

*

# Forty-Two

# DANGEROUS TEMPTATIONS: A CAUTIONARY TALE

*But my people would not listen to me; Israel would not submit to me. So I gave them over to their stubborn hearts to follow their own devices.*

Psalm 81:11–12

Here is a solemn word from the Lord. If we fight against God, He will eventually give us over to our own desires. If we insist on going our own way, in the end God will grant our request—often to our own eternal regret. A stubborn spirit whittles away at our faith as hard times eventually wear us down. Little by little we lose the joy we once had. Under pressure we begin to give in to bad habits or wrong attitudes, and then we begin the long slide in the wrong direction.

Not long ago a woman sat in my office and told me the saddest story I have heard in many years. She was raised as a Christian and at one time had a strong faith in Jesus Christ. But during a period of loneliness, she fell in with a bad crowd and began to dabble in sin, a little here and a little there. Eventually she began to experiment with drugs. Today she is hooked on heroin, so much so that she has resorted to terrible extremes in order to finance her drug habit. But when she is high, do you know what she does? She begins to talk about God. In my office we quoted Bible verses together.

She wants to be free, but the pain of coming off heroin is so great that she cannot face it. At one point I told her that if she didn't make the decision to come clean, it wouldn't be long before I spoke at her funeral. Then I challenged her to become a woman of truth because the truth would set her free. My parting words were the words of Jesus, "Go now and leave your life of sin" (John 8:11). She smiled and thanked me and said she needed to go and get some heroin or she wouldn't make it through the day. Then she walked out of my office.

I don't know what will happen to her. In the end, no one can make her decisions for her. Her story illustrates many truths, including the fact that simply having Bible knowledge cannot save a person from the consequences of wrong decisions. A few years ago she gave in to Satan's temptations—first in small ways, then in large ones—and now her life is almost destroyed. She is not yet thirty years old.

What happened to her can happen to any of us if we respond wrongly to hard times. Let no one condemn her, but instead let us consider our own lives and realize how vulnerable we are to Satan's attacks.

*Lord, when I am tempted to look down on others, help me to remember that "there but for the grace of God go I." May I never take Your protection for granted. Amen.*

—✳—

## A MOMENT'S REFLECTION

Can you think of a time when you wished for something—only to regret it later? Where are you currently vulnerable to Satan's attacks? Where do you feel that you are strong, and thus you might be vulnerable to Satan's attacks?

---

✳

# Forty-Three

# CONFESSION: NO MORE BLAMING OTHER PEOPLE

*Then I acknowledged my sin to you and did not cover up my iniquity. I said, "I will confess my transgressions to the Lord"—and you forgave the guilt of my sin.*

Psalm 32:5

Confession may be good for the soul, but it's not an easy step to take. Psalm 32 shows us what happens when we take the courage to admit our wrongdoing and to cry out to God for His mercy. Note the key phrase: "I . . . did not cover up my iniquity." You can cover up—and live riddled with inner guilt—or you can come clean with God and be made clean inside and out.

Some people would rather cover up than clean up. There is a reason that we're so good at the blame game. We make excuses because excuse making is in our family tree. It's part of our spiritual bloodstream. When we pass the buck, we're only doing what our ancestors did.

Let's roll the tape backward to the Garden of Eden and focus our lens right after Adam and Eve have eaten the forbidden fruit. To the untrained eye, it still looks like Paradise. Adam has just eaten the fruit and a silly, guilty grin slides across his face. He knows he has done something wrong, but he has no idea what is about to happen next.

Sin first brings shame. And with shame comes the disgrace of being uncovered. Then a strange sound of footsteps. Who could it be? It's the Lord walking in the garden in the cool of the day. Instinctively (and I use that word carefully), Adam and Eve hide themselves. Why? Who told them to hide? No one had to tell them anything. Their guilty consciences condemned them. Disobedience is now bearing its bitter fruit. Where once they enjoyed unbroken fellowship with God, now sin has separated them from their Creator.

But the truth is about to come out. "Have you eaten from the tree that I commanded you not to eat from?" "The woman you put here with me—she gave me some fruit from the tree, and I ate it." That's a classic piece of buck-passing. Blame it on the woman, and, if that doesn't work, blame it on God. Minimize your guilt by making someone else look bad.

That explains many things. First, it tells us that the tendency to blame others is deeply ingrained in human nature. Second, it tells us that left to ourselves, we will do anything to avoid taking personal responsibility for our actions. Third, it tells us that blaming others is often nothing more than a subtle twisting of the truth in order to take the heat off ourselves. Fourth, it tells us that without a deep working of the grace of God within us, we will do exactly what Adam and Eve did.

*Lord, I pray to be set free from the need to blame others for my own foolish actions. Amen.*

—— ✳ ——

## A MOMENT'S REFLECTION

Do you agree that honest confession is good for the soul? Why, then, is it so hard to do? Are you still blaming other people for your problems?

*Forty-Four*

---
✳
---

# CONVICTIONS:
# NO COMPROMISE
# WITH EVIL

*Men of perverse heart shall be far from me; I will have nothing to do with evil.*

Psalm 101:4

Several years ago *Newsweek* magazine called this "the Age of Enlightenment Skepticism." That simply means that we live in a world that no longer believes in truth. In another day men and women argued passionately about the truth; today we argue whether truth even exists, and if it does, how can anyone know the truth? We are no longer sure as a culture how to determine right from wrong —or even if we should make the effort. Many believe that truth exists in the eye of the beholder — "That's true for you but not necessarily for me." Truth becomes an entirely private affair with no implications for society at large.

Against that growing trend we have these solemn words of David. They remind us that many false teachers are themselves the very spirit of untruth. These "men of perverse heart" deny the very concept of truth—and they travel from place to place peddling their spiritual poison. Christians must reject such teachers—to the point of refusing them any sort of personal welcome. If we do welcome them, we are guilty of sharing in their evil deeds.

Strong words indeed—but greatly needed in this day of immense spiritual confusion. There are times when believers must aggressively oppose and refute false teaching and false teachers. To do less is to traffic with the enemies of the Cross and make a mockery of everything we believe.

These are exceedingly strong words, and one can wonder why David should feel impressed to write so bluntly. I think I know the answer. The longer we condone error, the easier it is to compromise. Little by little we become conditioned to moral decline and intellectual apostasy until it no longer seems so wrong to us.

What we do not oppose, we tolerate.
What we tolerate, we accept.
What we accept, we praise.
What we praise, we practice.

It may not happen overnight. In fact, the process of spiritual decline may take its course over the years, the decades, and the generations, but in the end the bills come due for not standing for the truth.

Most of us know the famous illustration about the frog in the kettle. Put a frog in a kettle with cold water and the frog will sit contentedly. Now slowly turn up the heat a few degrees at a time. Because the frog's system has time to adjust, he doesn't notice the changing temperature. When the water finally reaches a boil, the frog senses danger and tries to jump out, but it's too late. His legs won't move anymore.

Something like that happens to us when we coddle evil instead of facing it head-on and calling it what it is. When we refuse to oppose that which is wrong, in the end evil doesn't look so bad.

*Lord, make me so sensitive to You that I will be sensitive to sin. I want to love what You love and hate what You hate. Amen.*

— ✳ —

## A MOMENT'S REFLECTION

In what ways have you become "desensitized" to sin either in your own life or as it exists in society at large? What steps do you need to take in this area? Pray for discernment and for moral courage to do the right thing.

---

✳

---

# Forty-Five

# LOVING THE TRUTH:
# IT'S A DOUBLE-EDGED
# SWORD

*I hate and abhor falsehood but I love your law.*

Psalm 119:163

"Love and hatred are the leading affections of the soul; if those be fixed aright, the rest move accordingly." So said Matthew Henry more than three hundred years ago. You can tell a lot about a person by knowing what he loves—and what he hates. If you love God's Word, you must of necessity hate that which is opposed to God's truth.

Not long ago I did a brief survey of how we are to respond to false teachers. Here is what I found. We are to:

1. Guard against them—Acts 20:31
2. Have no fellowship with them—Ephesians 5:11
3. Avoid them—Romans 16:17
4. Reject them—Titus 3:10
5. Refute them—Titus 1:9
6. Refuse them—2 John 7–11

One question might be raised at this point: How can we reach an unsaved person if we must reject him outright? That's a good question. Here's the answer: These warnings are directed at false teachers, not confused people. Most of the unsaved people around us could not be called "false teachers." The vast majority (well over 90 percent, I would say) are so confused that they hardly know what they believe, much less are able to explain it to anyone else.

This is not a warning about spending time with confused people. Not at all. But it is a warning against spending too much time with those people who have given themselves over to the promotion of false doctrine and/or moral evil. When we find such a person, we are not to support him in any way. Let me make that stronger. We are not to support, encourage, or in any other way encourage those who teach, spread, or promote falsehood or moral evil.

The application of that truth is simple: We have to live in a fallen world, but we don't have to support things we know are wrong.

We need discernment lest we end up supporting heresy! Many today want:

- God but not Jesus
- Jesus but not Jesus only
- Jesus but not Jesus the Son of God
- A Jesus of their own making
- A buddy, a pal, a friend . . . but not the sovereign Lord
- A good example but not an Eternal Lord
- A multicultural gospel that promises everyone will go to heaven

155

- Religion but not a relationship with Jesus Christ
- An end to dogma and strong Bible doctrine
- To bring non-Christian religions to a level equal with Christianity
- To do away with sin, judgment, and eternal hell
- Do-it-yourself Christianity but not the Christianity of the Bible

We must be aware of these tendencies, and we must actively oppose those who promote them. Matthew Henry once more: "The more we see of the amiable beauty of truth the more we shall see of the detestable deformity of a lie."

*Lord God, I pray for a heart of love fully grounded in the truth of Your Word. Amen.*

— ✳ —

## A MOMENT'S REFLECTION

Take a few minutes to check out the various Bible verses regarding false teachers. Why does the Bible give so much specific instruction in this area? What happens in local churches (and denominations) when this truth is ignored?

# LOVE MUST HAVE LIMITS: ASKING HARD QUESTIONS

*If only you would slay the wicked, O God! Away from me, you bloodthirsty men!*

Psalm 139:19

It is altogether too easy to skip over this verse as simply one more unpleasant outburst. After speaking so beautifully about God's presence everywhere (vv. 7–12) and of His creative care of the unborn child (vv. 13–16), and after praising the vastness of God's thoughts (vv. 17–18), why would the psalmist, apparently without warning, shift gears into an attack on his enemies (vv. 19–22)? If the shift seems abrupt, perhaps it is because we do not understand that love must have limits. Loving the Lord of necessity means hating those who hate the Lord. (Verse 21 says this explicitly.)

These are strong words, but entirely true. Not every unbeliever "hates" the Lord, but some do, and their malice must not be underestimated or overlooked.

As a practical way of applying this truth, here are some questions we ought to ask ourselves:

1. Do I really believe the gospel of Jesus Christ?
2. In what areas of my life am I guilty of supporting

that which I know is wrong?

3. Have I been silent about evil when I should have been outspoken for the truth?

4. Have I been slowly lowering my standards of right and wrong in order to maintain friendships or to gain some personal advantage?

5. Have I been dabbling in falsehood when I really need to speak up for the truth?

6. Is there a relationship in my life that needs to be broken because it is dragging me down spiritually?

7. If my friends at church could see me during the week, would they be embarrassed by the things I do and say? Would Jesus be embarrassed?

Not easy questions, but ones we need to ask.

Love must have limits. We must love people, but we must not thereby tolerate false doctrine or condone moral evil. To use a familiar phrase, we must love the sinner while hating the sin. Sometimes we may appear to love the sinner too much, and sometimes we may appear to hate the sin too much. Both will be necessary if we are to stand for Christ and win the lost in this evil day.

Perhaps in our tolerance we have become indifferent to truth. When it comes to eternal issues, there is no room for neutrality. Not every issue is an eternal issue. We can have our own opinions in politics, sports, entertainment, and the latest news of the day. But some things are not up for grabs in the spiritual realm.

Set limits. Ask hard questions. Love God. Hate His

enemies. Pray for them—and for yourself that you will maintain a proper attitude.

> *O Lord, I pray for spiritual balance that I might love the sinner while rejecting the sin that sends sinners to hell. Help me to hope for the best while hating that which destroys the soul. Amen.*

—— ✳ ——

## A MOMENT'S REFLECTION

How would you answer the seven questions in this entry? In practical terms, how can we "love the sinner and hate the sin" at the same time? Name several spiritual truths that are not "up for grabs."

---

※

# Forty-Seven

# EVANGELISM: SPEAKING THE TRUTH IN LOVE

*Then I will teach transgressors your ways, and sinners will turn back to you.*

Psalm 51:13

As David considered the lessons he had learned following his tragic affair with Bathsheba, he vowed to God that he would use his experience to cause sinners to return to the Lord. This is the heart of evangelism—telling others what Christ has done for us. Until we have personally experienced God's pardoning grace, the gospel is to us only a theoretical message. But let a person declare how God rescued him in his moment of helpless desperation, let him speak openly of how he despaired of ever finding peace with God, and let him tell how Jesus found him, lifted him up, forgave his sins, gave him a new life, and set his feet in a new direction—let him tell that from his heart, and people will listen, because there is no testimony like the simple truth of a changed life. Converted sinners make the best preachers, because they know the truth of what they are saying.

Consider how Jesus dealt with people. He loved sinners and felt comfortable around them. He routinely went places and spent time with people in ways that many of us personally wouldn't care to do. (That statement says something about many modern Christians. We fall far short of Christ's compassion for the lost.) He welcomed everyone and turned no one away. He encouraged every genuine seeker who crossed His path. And He answered most of their questions—the good and the bad, the honest and the insincere. But that same Jesus also rebuked the Pharisees, cleared out the temple courtyard with a whip, and repeatedly spoke hard truth to powerful people without the slightest regard for His own safety.

What was He like? John 1:14 tells us that He was "full of grace and truth." What a wonderful phrase that is. He was perfectly balanced at all times between truth and love.

We face the same challenge today: to balance truth and love in all our relationships. We are to know the truth and to walk in love—all the time.

If we emphasize only the truth, we risk becoming hard and mean-spirited. That will only alienate other believers and turn away the lost from Christ.

If we emphasize only love, we risk becoming soft and sentimental. That soon leads us to compromise the gospel, excuse sin, and welcome evildoers.

Somehow—though it isn't easy—we must speak the truth in love. When we do, we will see sinners converted and transgressors returning to God.

*O God, I fall so far short of loving people as Jesus did. Create in me the mind and heart of Christ that I might live and love as He did. Amen.*

— ✳ —

## A MOMENT'S REFLECTION

In what ways did Jesus demonstrate a perfect balance between truth and love? Are you more likely to emphasize the truth part or the love part? How has Jesus changed your life in this area?

*Forty-Eight*

———— ✳ ————

# BOLD FAITH:
# SPEAK UP FOR GOD

*When I called, you answered me; you made me bold and stouthearted.*

Psalm 138:3

A friend's job of many years is about to come to an end in circumstances that are less than ideal. Her Christian faith is one of the unspoken issues. Certain powerful people wish she would leave of her own accord, but for the moment she intends to keep her job as long as she can. What should she do in the meantime?

Dr. Bob Jones Sr. was fond of saying, "The door of opportunity swings on the hinges of opposition." The apostle Paul certainly found that true in his own ministry. In 2 Corinthians 11:23–28 he reflected on his own difficulties as a preacher of the gospel. His list includes being flogged five times, beaten with rods three times, and stoned once. In Philippi he and Silas were stripped, beaten, and jailed. In Thessalonica his opponents literally ran him out of town. He speaks of being constantly on the move, of being in danger from bandits and from his own countrymen, of plots against him by the Gentiles and even by those he called "false brothers"—turncoats who used their Christian faith as a cover for treachery. "I have labored and toiled and have often gone without sleep; I have known hunger and thirst and have often gone without food; I have been cold and naked" (v. 27).

What was Paul's response to all this? "We dared to tell you his gospel in spite of strong opposition" (1 Thessalonians 2:2). The King James Version says, "We were bold in our God." What is boldness? It is important to remember that the gospel ministry is rarely easy or popular. For every person who receives us gladly, many more will have nothing to do with us. If we are waiting to win the world by acclamation, it isn't going to happen. Jesus said, "If the world hates you, keep in mind that it hated me first" (John 15:18). Sooner or later those words will come true for all the servants of God.

What should we do in the face of opposition or indifference?

1. Refuse to be intimidated.
2. Keep on praying.
3. Keep on keeping on.

Paul just kept on preaching. If they listened, that was good. If they didn't, that was too bad. If they opposed him, he didn't stop. If they attacked him, he kept on going.

In the case of my friend whose job may soon come to an end, she intends to be a positive witness for Christ wherever she is. Sometimes the best thing you can do is to keep on doing what you are already doing whether anyone pays attention or not. If you keep doing right long enough, sooner or later it will pay off.

*Father of lights, I ask not to be put in an easy situation; I ask rather for the strength to let my light shine right where I am. Amen.*

— ✳ —

## A MOMENT'S REFLECTION

Why do opportunity and opposition so often go together? What encouragement can you draw from Paul's sufferings for Christ? Pray for boldness in telling others of Christ today.

*Forty-Nine*

---
✳
---

# UNPOPULAR TRUTH: THERE IS NO SUBSTITUTE FOR THE WORD OF GOD

*Though the arrogant have smeared me with lies, I keep your precepts with all my heart.*

Psalm 119:69

Well-meaning church members sometimes encourage pastors not to speak out boldly about sin in their community because in so doing they risk turning away the very people the church is trying to reach. I understand that concern and to some extent I share it. I think that every godly pastor struggles to find the right balance between proclaiming the love of God and standing strong for the truth of God.

And let's be completely honest about it. No one likes to be unpopular. That's no fun. It would be better if everyone loved us. But they don't. If some people despise us for telling the truth about sin, then so be it.

Certain unchangeable facts are true and must be believed if we are to be truly Christian. These truths are not like the shifting tides of human opinion. They do not change with the latest Gallup Poll. These truths make Christianity what it is; if they are neglected or denied, then our faith loses its foundation.

Our only basis of authority is the Bible. Like Martin Luther at the Diet of Worms, we say, "Our conscience is bound by the Word of God. Here we stand. We can do no other."

Let me sharpen the point just a bit. Suppose someone were to ask why you are a Christian. It is not enough to say, "I believe in Jesus because He solves all my problems," or "I come to this church because I meet so many nice people here." That's beside the point. We must not claim to be Christians simply because of some advantage we receive. We must believe because the message is from God and is therefore true. No other answer will suffice. Like the campfire song says, "No turning back, no turning back." Believing the Bible is serious business. It matters not if arrogant people smear us with their lies. It happened in Bible times and it still happens today. Will you keep God's precepts with all your heart?

On a recent trip to downtown Chicago, I happened to see a beat-up blue church van parked on the street. It was from a church in a tough part of the city. As I looked I noticed the most unusual slogan I have ever seen on a church van. Under the name of the church were these words: "There is no substitute for the Word of God."

It's not very catchy but it's true. Since there is no substitute for the Word of God, our job is to preach it to everyone who will listen. Do your part and God Himself will take care of your reputation.

*Heavenly Father, Your Word is truth without any mixture of error. Grant that I might grow in the Word. Make it the foundation of my life. Amen.*

— ✳ —

## A MOMENT'S REFLECTION

Name five doctrines that you consider to be fundamental and non-negotiable. What are some modern-day substitutes for the Word of God? Why is it not enough to say "I believe in Jesus because He solves my problems"?

*Fifty*

---
✳
---

# GOD'S ENEMIES: THEY WON'T LAST FOREVER

*May God arise, may his enemies be scattered; may his foes flee before him.*

Psalm 68:1

M any of us feel uncomfortable with the notion that God has enemies. If God is a God of love (and He is), how can He have enemies? The answer is that God is not only a God of love, He is also a God of justice. And He doesn't take it lightly when people He created turn against Him.

Consider these facts:

Fact # 1: God's enemies will be scattered.
Fact # 2: God's enemies don't understand Fact # 1.
Fact # 3: God's people rejoice in Fact # 1.

We may stumble at the word enemies. But it's in the Bible. God takes it personally when people turn away from Him. We live in a day when few people will speak of God's anger toward sinners. We risk being called intolerant if we suggest that God has any enemies. Yet He does. Those who turn away from Him are His enemies. Those who fight against His truth are His enemies. Those who attack His people are God's enemies.

God sticks up for His own, God fights against His enemies, and God doesn't bless His opposition. Against the moral relativism of this day, we must plainly say that not everyone is going to heaven. Not everyone is a child of God. Not everyone will be saved. Many will, but many won't.

Psalm 68:1–2 uses three words to describe what happens to God's enemies.

1. They are scattered. (Their power is broken. Their alliances are smashed. Their armies are routed.)
2. They flee. (They run from God's judgment, and all their works are destroyed.)
3. They will perish. (They suffer in eternal torment in hell.)

In an anything-goes age, Psalm 68 reminds us that when it comes to God, He stays and His enemies go.

Do we truly believe these solemn and awesome words? Do we believe that God's enemies will one day be destroyed? Perhaps we should ask the question another way: Do we believe that God's enemies will one day perish in everlasting hell? Do these words affect our hearts as we consider the lost people around us? They are standing on thin ice right now, suspended only by the grace of God. The worst sinners who curse God must use the air He provided to curse His name.

Should these verses not also break our hearts? Should they not sober us, humble us, and force us to our knees? Must we not do everything in our power to save as many people as possible? If we gloat over the fate of the wicked, if we rejoice in the death of the wicked, then we do not have the heart of God. God takes no pleasure in the death of the wicked. He punishes them, He destroys them, He scatters them, but He does it with a broken heart.

Do we have the heart of God even for His enemies?

*Lord Jesus, I find it all too easy to hate my enemies and to wish the worst upon them. Teach me to love the people I want to hate so that I might share Your love with them. Amen.*

—— ✳ ——

## A MOMENT'S REFLECTION

Are you uncomfortable with the thought that God has enemies? Who are His enemies today? Take a moment to pray for God's enemies that through Jesus Christ they might become His friends.

171

Section Six
# LESSONS FROM LIFE

*Teach me your way, O Lord, and I will walk in your truth.*

Psalm 86:11

✳

# Fifty-One

# CREATION: GOD'S CALLING CARD

*The heavens declare the glory of God; the skies proclaim the work of his hands.*

Psalm 19:1

Suppose you were to visit my home while I was not there. How much could you learn about me and my family just by looking around? The moment you walked in you might suspect we had lived for a while in Texas because our living room has a southwestern flavor. If you noticed the painted egg from Russia and the mahogany from Haiti, you might guess that we have visited other countries. Although you might not know I was a pastor, you would certainly know I study the Bible from seeing all the Bibles and commentaries strewn around the computer in the corner of our dining room. You would soon learn that we have boys and that they love football and baseball. You'd even learn their favorite team from the pennant on the wall. By counting the beds you would figure out that we probably have three boys. And if you looked for girls' clothing you wouldn't find any. If you looked in my closet, you'd discover I'm tall by looking at my suits.

There's a lot more a careful observer could discover about the Pritchard family by rummaging through our drawers and bookshelves. In the end, you'd know a great deal about me although you wouldn't know me personally. The clues are all over my house for those who care to look.

This world is God's house. He has left clues everywhere about what kind of God He is. When you stand at the Grand Canyon, you can't help but be overwhelmed at the mighty power of God to create such magnificence. He must have had a mighty hand to scoop out the Royal Gorge in Colorado. He is as infinite as the dark recesses of the mighty Atlantic Ocean. Each snowflake testifies to His uniqueness. The changing colors of the Great Smoky Mountains proclaim His creativity.

The galaxies shout out, "He is here." The wildflowers sing together, "He is here." The rippling brooks join in, "He is here." The birds sing it, the lions roar it, the fish write it in the oceans—"He is here." All creation joins to sing His praise. The heavens declare it, the earth repeats it, and the wind whispers it—"He is here." Deep cries out to deep, the mighty sequoia tells it to the eagle who soars overhead, the lamb and the wolf agree on this— "He is here."

No one can miss the message. God has left His fingerprints all over this world. Truly, "This is my Father's world," and every rock, every twig, every river, and every mountain bears His signature. He signed His name to everything He made. The earth is marked "Made By God" in letters so big that no one fails to see it.

*Creator of the universe, give me eyes to see Your handiwork, ears to hear Your voice, and lips to proclaim Your greatness. Amen.*

— ✴ —

## A MOMENT'S REFLECTION

If someone visited your home in your absence, what could they learn about you just by looking around? What can people learn about God by looking at His universe? If the evidence is so plain, why do some people doubt the existence of God?

---
\*
---

# Fifty-Two

# THE NATIONS: UNDERSTANDING GOD'S FOREIGN POLICY

*Why do the nations conspire and the peoples plot in vain?*

Psalm 2:1

The Bible says much about the nations of the world—their origin, their alliances, their political power, their military might, their ultimate destiny. It reminds us again and again that the nations derive their strength from God—and that without Him they are nothing. They are, in fact, like a drop of water in a full bucket to Him (Isaiah 40:15).

That raises an interesting question: Does God have a foreign policy? The answer is yes. Does God care what the nations do? Yes. Does He pay attention to world leaders? Yes. Does He take their threats seriously? Yes. Psalm 2 shows us God's foreign policy. It is good to know in times like these.

The first few verses remind us that the world has always been an enemy of God. The nations "rage" (KJV), the rulers "plot in vain," planning their attack on the Almighty, who scoffs at their puny plans. He answers them by installing His Son as King over the entire earth. Someday all the nations will bow in submission before Jesus Christ. Philippians 2:9–11 echoes this truth with its promise that "every knee should bow . . . and every tongue confess that Jesus Christ is Lord, to the glory of God the Father."

Meanwhile God invites world rulers to "kiss the Son"—to bow in humble submission at His feet. Rebels will be judged, but God's children will be kept safe in the Day of Judgment.

The closing verses of Psalm 2 remind us that every nation will eventually bow before Jesus Christ the King. This ought to engender great confidence and form a ground for believing prayer. Since man left to himself always turns away from God, we should not be surprised to find ourselves in a minority position in society. Although we ought to do what we can to improve the world, we must not put our final trust in politicians or political parties. Today the nations rage; tomorrow the King comes to judge them. Between now and then, "blessed are all who take refuge in him" (v. 12).

Psalm 2 calls the church back to its central mission:

1. Personal submission to Jesus as Lord.
2. Proclamation of the gospel to every nation.
3. Growing confidence in God in the midst of increasing chaos on earth.

Let's lift up Jesus as the only hope of the world. And let's invite the rebels to put down their weapons and join us in the great celebration of God's Son, the Anointed One, our coming King—Jesus Christ.

*Omnipotent God, the nations are but a drop in the bucket to You. Open my eyes to see beyond the headlines to the hurting hearts in every land. Amen.*

## A MOMENT'S REFLECTION

What evidence suggests that the rulers of the world "rage" against God and against His Son? Why does God laugh when human rulers unite against Him? Take a few moments to thank God that He sits enthroned above the chaos of the nations.

---

# Fifty-Three

# HISTORY: REMEMBERING WHAT GOD HAS DONE

*He rebuked the Red Sea, and it dried up; he led them through the depths as through a desert.*

Psalm 106:9

We serve a God who has acted in history. He is not a theoretical God dreamed up by some mystic, nor is He a God cut off from this world. No, He has revealed Himself over and over again in human history by acting on behalf of His people. History really is His story.

Since God has acted in history, we can be sure that our faith rests on facts. Paul said to King Agrippa that Christ's life, death, and resurrection were not "done in a corner" (Acts 26:26), meaning, "O king, you don't have to take my word for it. Check it out for yourself. The facts are there for anyone to see." That's why the best answer to a skeptic is simply: Read the Bible and make up your own mind. "We did not follow cleverly invented stories when we told you about the power and coming of our Lord Jesus Christ, but we were eyewitnesses" (2 Peter 1:16). Likewise, John declared, "That which was from the beginning, which we have heard, which we have seen with our eyes, which we have looked at and our hands have touched—this we proclaim concerning the Word of Life" (1 John 1:1).

We have nothing to fear from the critics of the Christian faith, because our faith is founded on the great realities of the Bible—a literal creation by the hand of God, the existence of Israel, the miracles of the Old Testament, the prophecies of the Messiah, the birth, life, death, and resurrection of Jesus Christ, and His ascension into heaven. These things were not done in a corner.

All history points us toward God the Father and His Son Jesus Christ. What is history? That question may be answered many ways, but this much is true: History is the story of the outworking of God's plan for the human race. All true history—like all true science, and like truth in every field—leads us back to God. The best historians are those who see the hand of God moving across the generations to accomplish His divine plan.

Our thanksgiving ought to focus on the concrete acts of God on our behalf. As you count your blessings, focus on what God has done. What specific prayers were answered? Can you remember desperate moments when God came through amazingly for you? Do you recall great fear that turned into great rejoicing? Have you seen Him part the Red Sea for you? Did He destroy a few kings on your behalf? The answer is always yes. Recalling those moments deepens your faith in God and gives you confidence to face the future without fear.

*O Lord, when I count my blessings, I quickly run out of fingers, but I never run out of blessings from above. I pray for a good memory of the good things You have done for me. Amen.*

———✳———

## A MOMENT'S REFLECTION

It's count-your-blessings time. Give yourself five minutes and jot down every blessing you can remember from the last thirty days. Then thank God that His blessings are greater than your memory.

# Fifty-Four

# WORK:
# ANOTHER WAY TO
# SHARE YOUR FAITH

*Then man goes out to his work, to his labor until evening.*
Psalm 104:23

Work is a blessing, not a curse. Since most of our life is spent working to earn our bread, we ought to see our work as an extension of our worship of God. If we cannot be holy at our work, it is useless to attempt being holy elsewhere. Someone has said, "It is a terrible thing for religious people to have nothing to do but be religious." And again, "Those who get up in the morning with nothing to do but be religious are generally a great nuisance." It is the man who gets up in the morning and goes to his job and works all day in the marketplace, it is the woman who pursues her daily tasks at home or in the workplace with cheerfulness—these are the ones who make an impact for Christ in the world.

How we work is as crucial as how we pray. There is no greater testimony than the Christian mechanic at his bench, the Christian teacher in the classroom, the Christian secretary at the desk, the Christian nurse at the hospital, or the Christian accountant keeping the books.

This is where Christianity must be seen. Going to church means little if you are a lazy goldbrick on the job. Our problem is that we don't see our daily work as a way to worship God. But it is. What you do on Monday is just as important in the eyes of the Lord as what you do in church on Sunday.

Let me state it negatively and positively. On the negative side, "Don't be lazy and give the church a black eye." On the positive side, "You can make the church beautiful by the way you do your job."

Remember, you are the only Bible someone will ever read. You are the only gospel someone will ever hear. You are the only Christian someone will ever meet. What do people read, hear, and see when they look at your life?

The lowliest occupation becomes a powerful sermon when it is done with dignity, propriety, honesty, diligence, and faithfulness. The common man who does his common job with uncommon grace will never lose his self-respect and will win respect for the church of Jesus Christ.

Someone has said it this way: "The only way to show that Christianity is the best of all faiths is to show that it produces the best of all men." When we Christians show that our faith makes us better workers, truer friends, better neighbors, kinder men and women, then we are really preaching.

Our lives are sermons that daily draw others to Jesus —or push them away from Him.

*God of all my days, make me a hard worker who needs not to be ashamed. When I am tempted to be lazy, remind me that You are always watching me. Let my work be my worship today. Amen.*

——— ✳ ———

## A MOMENT'S REFLECTION

Do you agree that your work is a major part of your spiritual witness? Have you ever known a Christian who gave a poor testimony because of poor work habits? Take a moment to pray that your work will be an effective "sermon" today.

---
*

# Fifty-Five

# CHILDREN: A HANDFUL AND A QUIVERFUL

*Blessed is the man whose quiver is full of them [sons]. They will not be put to shame when they contend with their enemies in the gate.*

Psalm 127:5

This verse seems to teach that large families are a special sign of God's blessing. How full is "full"? The Bible doesn't say, but in every place it speaks to the subject, children are a sign of God's favor. Not all Bible families were large, of course, but many were. This goes against the flow of much that is taught today, but the notion of having fewer children so that you can spend more money on them or because you can love each child more would seem quite foreign to the writers of the Bible.

The city gate was the place where men of power and influence conducted their business. It was also the place where wise men ruled and made judgments. Men would meet their adversaries "in the gate." A father with many sons thus had many defenders when he was falsely accused. They could stand and testify to his good name. Note that nothing is said about money or power or position. God's blessing is not seen in worldly wealth or the accumulation of "things" but in a happy family that rallies to the call whenever trouble comes.

Here is a striking contrast between a workaholic husband who stays on the road seven days a week and is absent in spirit even when he is home. What shall it profit a man if he gains the whole world and yet loses his own family? I know many men who spend sixty to seventy hours per week on the job, then in a quiet moment they confide they wish they could spend more time at home. Years later they realize they had all the time they needed, but they used it for other things. Oh, to be wise enough to learn this while there is still time to make a difference.

Derek Kidner makes a useful point when he reminds us that raising children can be tiresome and difficult. It is not, he says, untypical of God's gifts that they are liabilities before they become assets. Children are both a burden and a blessing. The greater their promise, the more challenging will be the task of raising God's children. It is likely that our children will be a handful before they become a quiverful.

We can partner with the Lord Jesus Christ in the building of our homes. When we do, our families will be blessed, our children will prosper, our marriages will flourish, and Jesus Christ will be praised. And when we come to the end of the day, when all our work on earth is done, we may look back with joy and say, "God blessed us with a happy Christian family." There is no greater reward, no better testimony, no higher goal for Christian parents than a family that loves the Lord and each other.

If we can say that when the day is done, we may leave this world singing, knowing that we prevailed in the one area of life that matters the most.

> *O Lord, save me from working so long and so hard on my career than I lose my family. I want to work with You in building a happy Christian family. Amen.*

— ✳ —

## A MOMENT'S REFLECTION

Do you agree that children are a blessing from the Lord? Why are God's gifts often a liability before they become a blessing? If you have children, take a moment to pray for each one right now.

# Fifty-Six

# GODLY FRIENDS: COMPANIONS ON THE ROAD TO HEAVEN

*I am a friend to all who fear you, to all who follow your precepts.*

Psalm 119:63

Are you familiar with the term "cocooning"? Experts use it to describe contemporary American life. It refers to the fact that Americans are using their homes as a way to escape contact with the world. Cocooning is what happens when you use your home like a medieval castle. You let down the drawbridge, go to work, come home, cross the drawbridge, raise it, and fill the moat with water. You sit down, turn on the TV, read the paper, and then go to bed. The next day you do it all over again.

One result of cocooning is that people don't really get to know other people. They never let anyone get close enough. Only the special few get invited across the drawbridge. Everyone else is "Hi, how are you? Good to see you. Sorry I don't have time to talk. Gotta run. Bye-bye."

God never intended that His children live in cocoons. He designed Christian life not to be a solo, but a duet, a trio, a quartet, a quintet, a choir, and a mighty symphony. He intended that as you join your life with other people, they would help you and you would help them. It's not easy to live this way, because it runs against the grain of contemporary culture. Although we hunger for close relationships, we live in a way that makes it easier to keep things on a very superficial level. We move too much, we don't know how to talk to each other, we're too busy, and we're unwilling to commit ourselves to long-term relationships.

You may be struggling right now because you don't have a group, you're not close to anyone, and you're not accountable to anybody. God didn't create a race of hermits. He intended that His children would live together, and that in living together, they would help each other along the way. It is God's will that we live together as brothers and sisters in a family relationship so that we can love each other, encourage each other, admonish each other, hug each other, pick each other up when we fall down, rejoice together, weep together, and correct each other when we make mistakes.

How is it with you? Do you have a few people in your life who really know you? Or do you always wear the mask, put on the costume, play the game, because the show must go on? Are you accountable to anybody for the way you live? Or are you doing it all by yourself?

*Lord God, thank You for the gift of Christian friends. Help me to be a friend to my friends today. Amen.*

## A MOMENT'S REFLECTION

How many truly close friends do you have? Which relationships are in need of some attention from you? What can you do about them this week?

——— ✳ ———

# Fifty-Seven

# STRANGERS IN A STRANGE LAND: THIS WORLD IS NOT MY HOME

*I am a stranger on earth; do not hide your commands from me.*

Psalm 119:19

I am writing these words in Miango, Nigeria, on the final night of a thirteen-day visit with some missionary friends. It doesn't take long to understand what it means to be a stranger in a strange land. You will never know what it's like until you visit a foreign country and there see people who don't look like you, talk like you, think like you, or live like you. They have a set of values you don't understand, a language you can't speak, and food you can't eat. You pick up the newspaper and you can't read it. You turn on the radio and it doesn't make sense. You're standing on a sidewalk and you can't communicate with the people who pass by. And no matter how friendly the people are, you never forget, not even for one second, that you are an outsider.

If you are a follower of Jesus, you have become a stranger—not in some other country but in your own hometown. It's like going back to the place where you grew up only to find out that everything has changed and nothing looks the same. You didn't move physically, but you did move spiritually. Salvation has made you a stranger in the world.

If you are a businessman and have decided as a Christian not to cheat, lie, or double-cross, if you've decided to deliver what you promise, you are a stranger in the world.

If you are a husband and you have decided to be faithful to your wife because you are a Christian, you are a stranger in the world.

If you are a Christian teenager, and you have decided to live for Jesus in the halls of your high school, you are a resident alien.

If you have decided to do your work as unto the Lord, not as pleasing men but in order to please God, if you have decided that money will not be the determining factor in your life, then you are a stranger in the world.

If you are working in an office where coarse language, profanity, and loose talk are the accepted norm and you have decided not to join in, you are a stranger in the world.

If any of those things are true, then welcome to the fraternal order of Christian strangers. You are an alien in this world because you are a citizen of heaven. Don't be discouraged if you sometimes feel out of place. Just remember you're not home yet.

*Lord of the cloud and fire, I am a pilgrim marching through the wilderness on my way to the Promised Land. When I am discouraged and want to go back to Egypt, keep my feet marching toward Canaan. Amen.*

— ✳ —

A MOMENT'S REFLECTION

In what sense are Christians "strangers in a strange land"? According to Philippians 3:20–21, where is your true citizenship? Name three evidences that you personally are a stranger in the world.

# Fifty-Eight

# GOD'S NAME:
# DON'T TAKE IT IN VAIN!

*Remember how the enemy has mocked you, O Lord, how foolish people have reviled your name.*

Psalm 74:18

The Third Commandment warns us that "the Lord will not hold anyone guiltless who misuses his name" (Exodus 20:7). Do you know what that means? It means that God is not a toy you can play with casually and then put back on the shelf. It's like those warning signs that say, "Danger! High Voltage!" If you ignore the sign, you will soon be electrocuted. Psalm 74:18 reminds us that God takes note of how His name is used—both by His friends and by His enemies. The foolish people who have reviled His name will soon learn that "God is a live wire" and His name is not to be taken lightly.

If that sounds strange, consider the story of Uzzah in 2 Samuel 6. King David had ordered that the ark of God be transported from the house of Abinadab into the city of Jerusalem. David's men put the ark of God—"which is called by the Name"—on a cart, which was their first mistake. God had ordered that the Levites should carry the ark by inserting long poles through rings on the sides. Perhaps they were in a hurry; perhaps they thought it didn't matter. Two sons of Abinadab—Ahio and Uzzah—walked beside the cart to guide it and to protect it. As they approached the threshing floor of Nacon, the oxen stumbled, causing the ark to sway on the cart. Uzzah immediately reached out his hand to steady the ark. It was the last act of his life. When he touched the ark, God struck him dead. "The Lord's anger burned against Uzzah because of his irreverent act; therefore God struck him down and he died there beside the ark of God" (2 Samuel 6:7).

Very possibly that seems like a huge overreaction to you. After all, Uzzah was only trying to do his job. But God was sending a message that no one should dare to trifle with His name. Enthusiasm must be accompanied by obedience. It's not enough to mean well. We've got to do the right thing.

Take God lightly . . . and you will die!

That's the message of Uzzah.

Are you surprised? Don't be. Don't the great celebrities pay millions to protect their names? Don't major corporations hire hundreds of attorneys to ensure their corporate name is not misused? Misuse a corporate symbol and you'll soon find yourself on the wrong end of a lawsuit.

God's name is important to Him. Misuse it and He'll see you in court!

*Sovereign Lord, You have warned me of the dangers of irreverence. Help me to take these words to heart. Amen.*

—✳—

## A MOMENT'S REFLECTION

Why is God's name so important to Him? List several ways people misuse God's name. What does the story of Uzzah tell us today?

*Fifty-Nine*

---
✳
---

# ANGELS: SUPERNATURAL PROTECTORS OF GOD'S CHILDREN

*Praise the Lord, you his angels, you mighty ones who do his bidding, who obey his word.*

Psalm 103:20

Who are the angels? They are spirit beings who serve God in heaven. Evidently they have many functions, including guarding the heavenly throne, praising God, doing battle with the demons, and protecting the people of God. Hebrews 1:14 calls them "ministering spirits" who are sent to serve the people of God. We should think of the angels of God ascending and descending Jacob's ladder in Genesis 28:12. Perhaps they take our prayers to heaven and bring God's answers back down to us.

Daniel 6:22 tells us that an angel shut the mouths of the lions. Acts 12 records that an angel rescued Peter in prison. Jesus told us that the angels in heaven rejoice when a sinner repents and comes to Christ (Luke 15:10). First Corinthians 11:10 seems to imply that angels carefully watch believers as they gather in worship. First Peter 1:12 says that they have an intense interest in everything related to our salvation. Matthew 18:10 speaks of little children and "their angels," a reference to guardian angels in heaven who watch over the people of God. Daniel 10 speaks of a great struggle in the unseen realm between the angels and the demonic forces of the devil. Second Kings 6 tells the dramatic story of Elisha and his servant at Dothan when they were surrounded by the armies of Aram. The servant was frightened until Elisha prayed that his eyes might be opened. Then he saw "the hills full of horses and chariots of fire all around Elisha" (v. 17).

The angels are closer to us than we think. Hebrews 12:22 says that in Christ we have come near to "thousands upon thousands of angels in joyful assembly." Just as God Himself is not far away, neither are His holy angels. They surround the people of God, watching us with great interest, observing our progress in the Christian faith, standing by to help us when we are in great distress. Sometimes they intervene in subtle ways, sometimes in dramatic, miraculous fashion to deliver God's people.

This subject is timely because the last few years have seen an explosion of interest in angels and their ministry. Even secular bookstores are filled with books about angels. Although much that has been written is fanciful, let us not forget that the Bible clearly speaks of angels and their crucial role in protecting God's people.

The fact that we do not see them does not mean they are not there. Without the angels of God, we would likely not survive another day. Thank God for the holy angels who deliver God's people in times of trouble.

*My Father, I thank You for the angels, those unseen messengers from heaven, who encamp around the righteous. Thank You for protecting me in ways I will never know until I finally get to heaven. Amen.*

A MOMENT'S REFLECTION

Name four ways that angels protect and help God's people. Read 2 Kings 6:8–17. What does that suggest about the angelic hosts who surround you today?

---

※

---

# Sixty

# GOD'S WORD: FOREVER SETTLED IN HEAVEN

*Your word, O Lord, is eternal; it stands firm in the heavens.*
Psalm 119:89

This verse demonstrates why the battle over the nature of the Bible is so crucial. If it is only the word of man, then it is changeable, fickle, and unreliable. But if the Bible is the Word of God, then it is utterly and completely authoritative. If God has spoken in the Bible, then what He says has final claim on my life.

Let me summarize this point with two simple statements:

1. If the Bible comes from man, we are entitled to sit in judgment on it.
2. If the Bible comes from God, we must bow in submission to it.

This is a crucial question: What do you believe about the Bible? Does it come from man or from God? Is it on the level with the daily newspaper, or does it speak with divine authority?

If you say it is the Word of God, then you must also

say that it is not simply one message among many. It is not like the Republican or the Democratic platform that come about through debate and consensus. If the Bible is the Word of God, it is utterly exclusive in its claims. It does not beg for our approval. The Word of God is not like the first draft of a thesis that the writer submits and asks, "What do you think?"

A friend in Texas sent me an E-mail saying that he had just received the first two chapters of his dissertation back from the seminary library. They covered his pages with red marks. Change this, delete that, follow a different form in your footnotes, use this kind of paper, indent this many spaces, and so on. He has to do what they say if he wants to get his degree.

Not so with the Bible. God never asks us to correct His Word. He never asks us to review Isaiah and make a few changes. And He won't abide by those who add to or take away from the book of Revelation (22:18–19).

It reminds me of the story of a church that was going through a difficult controversy. No one could agree on anything. At a business meeting one night the various factions were arguing about the minutes of the previous meeting. When the pastor read a passage of Scripture, an old man stood to his feet and said, "Mr. Chairman, I move that the Bible stand approved as read."

So it must be for you and me. The Bible stands approved as read, without correction, without change, without deletion, without addition.

*O Lord, may I never doubt Your Word, but simply believe it, obey it, and build my life upon it. Amen.*

——— ✳ ———

## A MOMENT'S REFLECTION

How do you know the Bible is the Word of God? Why is the doctrine of inerrancy (that the Bible is without error in all its details) so crucial for our faith? Spend some time thanking God for giving us the Bible.

Section Seven
# THE LONG ROAD HOME

*The Lord is my strength and my shield; my heart trusts in him, and I am helped.*
Psalm 28:7

# Sixty-One

# SANCTIFICATION: A FAINT SOUND ON THE INSIDE

*I cry out to God Most High, to God, who fulfills his purpose for me.*

Psalm 57:2

These are the words of a man who has been profoundly changed by God:

If I had asked a close friend sixteen years ago to write down a description of me and then done the same today, here is the conclusion you would come to once you read them: These are two distinctly different people with very little in common.

What happened? Nothing short of a miracle. I won't go into all the circumstances, but sixteen years ago I was at the end of my emotional and spiritual rope. One day I got down on my knees and told God to either change me or take me home because I didn't want to live another minute if my life was going to be the same as it had been. That's when I started to hear the faint sounds of hammering and sawing inside.

To jump to the end of the story, over the last sixteen

years God has created a whole new person inside this one. That's not visible to most folks. And it wasn't in the twinkling of an eye. But it is a miracle! It is spectacular! And it isn't over yet! What God has done in my life is more miraculous than if He had grown a new arm or leg to replace an amputated one—because He has grown a whole new person. He still does miracles! They are spectacular! They are in His time! To God be the glory!!

I love one particular sentence in that testimony: "That's when I started to hear the faint sounds of hammering and sawing inside." If you have been a believer for any length of time, you already know about that hammering and sawing in your own life. Theologians have a big word for that. They call it "sanctification." It's the work God does inside the heart of a believer in order to make him into a brand-new person. That leads me to offer a street-level definition of sanctification: It is everything God does in your life and mine to make sure we turn out right.

Sanctification is not some mystical, strange, emotional experience. Whenever you invest in someone's life, you care about how that person turns out. That's why parents care so much and worry so much about their children. They have given their lifeblood, and so it matters almost more than life itself how their children turn out. Now apply that same truth in the spiritual realm. God has invested in us the death of His only begotten Son. Sanctification is the divine guarantee that that investment will not be wasted. Sanctification, then, is God's commitment to us. We're going to make it. He will personally see to it.

*Father, I bless You that I am not what I used to be, though I am not yet everything I want to be. By Your grace I am not yet all that I am going to be. Amen.*

—— ✳ ——

## A MOMENT'S REFLECTION

Where have you sensed the "faint sound of hammering and sawing" in your life? What kind of "investment" has God made in His children? What guarantee do we have that He will finish His work in us?

---

### * ---

# Sixty-Two

# A FUTURE SALVATION: WE'RE NOT IN HEAVEN YET

*The Lord upholds all those who fall and lifts up all who are bowed down.*

Psalm 145:14

Perhaps you've heard the term "good enough for government work." That's a derisive (and somewhat unfair) way of saying, "Don't worry about the details. The joints don't have to fit, the margins can be crooked, and we don't need to worry about the budget. We don't have to be perfect; in fact, we don't even have to be close."

Mark it down plainly: God does not do shoddy work. Everything He does is perfect. But many of us feel like our lives are "government work." We look inside and see lots of good and bad mixed together and a whole bunch of loose connections and a lot of parts that don't seem to work right.

That's the way it is in a fallen world. We're stuck with what seems to be "government work" in this life. But it won't be that way forever. God has promised that in the end, we will be sanctified through and through.

We're not finished yet—but we will be.

We're not completely clean today—but we will be.

We're not wholly wise today—but we will be.

We're not totally redeemed right now—but we will be.

We're not always useful to God—but we will be.

John Calvin used a picturesque expression to describe what God is doing. God intends "the entire renovation of the man." I confess that I never understood renovation until I moved to Oak Park, Illinois, ten years ago. Now I know what it means because everything in this village is under constant renovation. Around here a "new" house is only seventy years old and an average house is eighty years old. An "old" house is at least a hundred years old.

Anyone who can renovate old buildings does a land office business in Oak Park. If you live in one of those houses, you never really get the job finished. First you work on the roof, then you start on the living room, then the kitchen, then the bedrooms one by one. Probably you'll have trouble with the plumbing and the electrical fixtures (more than once!). Eventually you've got to replace the porch, repaint the trim, and install a new heater and maybe even an air conditioner. You can work on a house for fifteen years and still not be completely finished. There's always something else to do.

If you think houses are hard, try renovating a human life. That's a job so tough only God would attempt it. Some of us take twenty-five years, some thirty, some forty, and many of us take fifty-plus years and the job still isn't done. I think God just eventually says to some people, "I've done all I can do down there. Come on up here and I'll finish the job where the working conditions are much better." (In truth, that's what He eventually says to all of us.)

Today we are holy in spots. When God is finished with us, we will be holy through and through.

*Holy Spirit, I long for the day when the renovation of my life will be complete. Until then, grant me faith to believe that the work continues even when I do not see it clearly. Amen.*

—✳—

## A MOMENT'S REFLECTION

If God intends the "entire renovation" of the redeemed person, why doesn't He do it all the moment we are saved? What are the advantages of gradual sanctification? Name three places where your life is in need of extensive renovation.

———— * ————

# Sixty-Three

# OBEDIENCE: GOD'S PATHWAY TO BLESSING

*Do good to your servant, and I will live; I will obey your word.*

Psalm 119:17

This verse presents grace and works in beautiful harmony. The first clause reminds us that it is only by God's goodness that any of us lives another day. It is God who gives us life, breath, and the blessings we enjoy moment by moment. Should He withdraw those gifts, none of us would live to see tomorrow. In the words of the Doxology, we live in dependence on God "from whom all blessings flow." If God should give us what we deserve, we would all immediately perish. Our hope rests in God's grace to us—that God will "do good" to us according to His abundant mercy.

The second clause points us to the only wise response to God's goodness—we should obey His word. Obedience means following orders whether you like them or not. As any soldier knows, you are to obey your superiors even when you don't understand why they want you to do a certain thing. Sometimes you'll figure it out later; often you won't. This applies in the spiritual realm as well.

When we adopt the habits, mannerisms, dress, speech, and distinctive traits of the world, we are covering up our true identity as God's children. We are believers masquerading in the costume of the world.

Don't do it. Let your life by its outward character demonstrate the inner change that Jesus Christ has made. That means there are things you shouldn't do, places you shouldn't go, and habits you shouldn't have. Obedience means letting go of anything that doesn't belong in a redeemed life.

We have been saved out of our sins. We ought to show it by the way we live. What is needed is a decisive choice to obey God every day. We will be exactly what we choose to be.

We know God, and God is holy. We ought to have a family resemblance that reflects our Father's basic character to the world. When I was a child, I often heard adults refer to me as "Dr. Pritchard's son." His reputation went along with me. I was expected to live up to my father's good name.

In the days of Alexander the Great, a soldier was charged and tried for desertion in battle. The emperor heard about it and called the young soldier in. He heard the charge and then he asked his name. The reply came back, "Alexander, sir." With that the emperor looked him sternly in the eye and said, "Soldier, change your behavior or change your name."

So it is that we bear the name of God everywhere we go. That ought to make a difference in the way we live.

*Lord of my life, give me grace to obey so that I will not hesitate but will do what You ask. Deliver me from the folly of using my lack of understanding as an excuse for disobedience. Amen.*

—✳—

## A MOMENT'S REFLECTION

In what practical ways are you completely dependent on God at this very moment? Are you guilty of incomplete obedience to God? If so, what do you plan to do about it?

---
※
---

# Sixty-Four

# SIN AND THE CHRISTIAN: MARTIN LUTHER'S COMMENT

*I confess my iniquity; I am troubled by my sin.*

Psalm 38:18

It isn't often that I have breakfast with a church historian, but it happened recently, and I learned something very useful. We shared bagels and cream cheese and discussed the theology of the Reformation—his specialty. In the course of our conversation he related a famous quote by Martin Luther. It is, he said, central to Luther's view of the spiritual life. It is one simple sentence filled with meaning: "The whole Christian life is a life of repentance."

As I thought about those words, I could not find anything to quarrel with. But the words seem strange to modern ears. Repentance is not a concept we like to think about. It implies guilt, which we would rather not admit, and it speaks of changing our ways and reforming our habits, which in the best of times is not easy to do. And perhaps some of us have been taught that repentance happens only once—the moment you become a Christian.

Although some people would like to deny this, both

the Bible and common sense unite to teach us that as long as we live in this fallen world, we will struggle with sin to one degree or another. But it is not just the fallen world that's a problem; our fallen nature also remains with us. In some sense our basic sinful nature remains a part of us even after we are born again. In the words of Luther once again, we are "simultaneously justified and sinful," righteous before God because of His imputed righteousness, but sinful in ourselves. Try as we might, we will never be completely rid of sin in this life.

The fact that sin remains with us till the day we die should not discourage us in the least. Only those who have mistakenly believed the claims of sinless perfectionism will be disappointed to discover that no one is sinless in this life. In the words of Anselm of Canterbury, one of the greatest of all the medieval theologians, "You have not yet considered how great your sin is."

Is there anything positive from the believer's continual struggle with sin? Yes. First, our struggles develop humility and kill pride. Second, they create a deep desire for the grace of God. Third, our struggles teach us the truth of John 15:5, that apart from a living relationship with Jesus Christ we have no power within us to defeat sin and live in righteousness.

Seen in that light, Martin Luther's comments make perfect sense. "The whole Christian life is a life of repentance." This is not negative but positive, because our repentance forces us to go back to the cross of Christ for the forgiveness we need.

*Lord Jesus, I long to be delivered from my bondage to sin. Grant that I might emerge victorious by Your power. Amen.*

## A MOMENT'S REFLECTION

Do you agree with Martin Luther's comment? Why is sinless perfection impossible in this life? Why would God allow us to be simultaneously just and sinful?

# Sixty-Five

# THE UNSTOPPABLE GOD: WHAT HE DOES LASTS FOREVER

*The Lord will fulfill his purpose for me; your love, O Lord, endures forever—do not abandon the works of your hands.*

Psalm 138:8

"Your love endures forever." This little phrase is all-important. It is the foundation for the doctrine of eternal security. It is often said that those who are saved are saved forever. How do we know this is true? We know it because God is faithful to keep His promises. Our entire hope—both in this life and in the life to come—rests on the faithfulness of God. His faithfulness bears the entire weight of our puny efforts. We are saved because of God—and not because of anything we do. He provides the grace that saves us, and He also gives us the faith to believe (Ephesians 2:8). He even gives us the Holy Spirit, who gives us the power to obey God.

"The Lord will fulfill his purpose for me." What is "His purpose" for His children? That He would take us where He finds us—as sinners—and that, justifying us even while we are still sinful (see Romans 4:5), He would set about the lifelong project of conforming us to the image of Jesus Christ (Romans 8:29).

All of us are works in progress. We're not finished, not glorified, not perfected, not completed. We're all "under construction." Construction is long, loud, noisy, and very messy. That's why most of us can hear the sound of hammering and sawing on the inside. God never stops His work because there is so much work that needs to be done. If you concentrate on your weakness, you will lose your confidence. If you concentrate on God's faithfulness, you will grow in confidence.

What makes us think that God will ever finish the job? In my mind's eye, I picture God as a sculptor working with a rough piece of marble. He's working on a big chunk named "Ray Pritchard." It's a hard job because the chunk is badly marred, misshapen, discolored, and cracked in odd places. It's about the worst piece of marble a sculptor could ever find. But God is undeterred, and He works patiently at His job, chipping away the bad parts, chiseling an image into the hard stone, stopping occasionally to polish here and there. One day He finally finishes one section of the statue. The next morning when He returns to the studio that section is messed up. "I thought I finished that yesterday," He says. "Who has been messing with My statue?"

It turns out that I'm the culprit. I'm my own worst enemy. What I thought would improve things has only messed them up.

But God is faithful. He patiently picks up His chisel and goes back to work. He won't quit halfway through a project. What God starts, He finishes. You can take that to the bank.

*Heavenly Father, grant me the gift of patience while I wait for You to finish Your work in me. Amen.*

— ✳ —

## A MOMENT'S REFLECTION

In what sense are you your own worst enemy? Name several parts of your life where you have seen real spiritual progress in the last several years. Ask God to continue molding you into the image of Jesus Christ.

---
※
---

# Sixty-Six

# HOLINESS:
# JUST SAY NO TO SIN

*Who may ascend the hill of the Lord? Who may stand in his holy place? He who has clean hands and a pure heart, who does not lift up his soul to an idol or swear by what is false.*

Psalm 24:3–4

These verses tell us that not everyone is welcome in God's presence. God welcomes those with clean hands and pure hearts. Those who have chosen a sinful lifestyle should think twice before coming glibly before the Lord. Dirty hands are not welcome in "his holy place."

When God says, "Be holy because I, the Lord your God, am holy" (Leviticus 19:2), in context it means "Be pure for I am pure" and "Be clean for I am clean" and especially "Be different for I am different."

Strange as it may seem, practical holiness begins with the negative. That is to say, holiness is more than what you do. It's also what you don't do.

It's more than where you go; it's also where you won't go.

It's more than what you say; it's also what you won't say.

It's more than what you watch on TV; it's also what

you won't watch.

It's more than the music you listen to; it's also the music you don't listen to.

It's more than what you wear; it's also what you won't wear.

It's more than what you worship; it's also what you won't worship.

It's more than who your friends are, it's also who your friends aren't.

It's more than who you sleep with; it's also who you don't sleep with.

It's more than what you do when you come to church on Sunday; it's also what you do when there's not a church member in sight.

Why should there be a negative emphasis? That's a good question. I can think of at least two answers. (1) When the world looks at us, the easiest difference to see is in the negative. (2) Until we are set apart from sin, we are not yet ready to be separated to God and His service.

Let us suppose that I ask my wife out for a special date and I tell her that we're going someplace nice. The appointed hour comes and I show up in dirty overalls, I stink, my hair is filthy, my hands are greasy, and my nose is running. Meanwhile, my wife is dressed in her prettiest outfit waiting for me. Now, will she go out with me? Yes or no? No, because I haven't shown proper respect for her. Does she still love me? Yes. But she's not going out with me like that. I can go, but if I do I'll be going alone.

I'm not ready to go out with her until I get cleaned up.

In the very same way, as long as my life is unclean I'm not ready to go anywhere with God. I haven't shown Him proper respect and honor. Does He still love me? Yes. But until my life is clean I'll be going out by myself.

*My Lord, make me holy as You are holy. You alone can answer this prayer. Amen.*

— ✴ —

## A MOMENT'S REFLECTION

Why does practical holiness begin with the negative? What happens when we neglect God's call to moral purity in the "small areas" of life? Pray for clean hands and a pure heart so that you can come before the Lord with a clear conscience.

※

# Sixty-Seven

# SOWING AND REAPING: GOD'S LAW OF THE HARVEST

*Those who sow in tears will reap with songs of joy. He who goes out weeping, carrying seed to sow, will return with songs of joy, carrying sheaves with him.*

Psalm 126:5–6

This is the Law of the Harvest. All farmers know that planting time is an act of faith. You take your seed, put it in the ground, and cover it with soil. You can't see a thing. One day passes—nothing. Two days pass—nothing. Three days pass—nothing. A week, two weeks— nothing. To the untrained eye, it seems that all your planting was for naught. The farmer may be tempted to think, *I wasted my time. Maybe I shouldn't have planted as much as I did.* It's always that way when you sow. You plant the seed and then you wait. Once the seed is in the ground, it's too late to change your mind. But if you wait long enough, the harvest comes. Then you are glad you planted as much as you did.

So it is with everything we do for the Lord. Evangelism is like sowing seeds. Not many people come to Christ the first time they hear the message. Like most of us, most people need to think about it, ponder it, ask a few questions, and only later trust Christ. Psalm 126:5–6 encourages us to believe that as we tell others about Christ in the power of the Holy Spirit, God will give the harvest of new believers in His own time and in His own way.

The same principle holds true for our giving, which often seems financially impossible. You've got bills to pay, a heavy mortgage, car payments, dental bills, school bills, maternity clothes to buy, child support payments you have to make. The pantry is almost bare, your youngest daughter needs a new dress, and the poodle needs a pedicure. It looks impossible. You want to give to the Lord, but it seems like throwing seed on the ground. Maybe you should go back. Maybe you should wait. Maybe you can give when you get another raise or when your spouse takes a second job.

Ah . . . but then comes the harvest. It's wonderful to live on a farm during harvest time. All the work of the year begins to pay off. Back from the field comes the truck loaded with corn or wheat or cotton or hay. You don't regret sowing all that seed at harvest time.

That is the great principle: What you give, you end up receiving. This applies in every area of the spiritual life. The generous man receives blessings from God all out of proportion to his own giving. God will be no man's debtor. Those who sow in tears will reap with songs of joy.

*Lord of the harvest, grant me the faith to sow in tears, knowing that in due time I shall reap a joyful harvest from Your hand. Amen.*

225

———— ✳ ————

## A MOMENT'S REFLECTION

Explain the Law of the Harvest. How does it apply to prayer? Bible study? Evangelism? Missions? Other areas of the Christian life?

---
\*

# Sixty-Eight

# RADIANCE: LEARNING TO WALK IN THE LIGHT

*For with you is the fountain of life; in your light we see light.*
Psalm 36:9

This verse contains a hugely important principle for the spiritual life. It tells us that all life and light comes from God and that only as we walk in His light will we see the light. Said a shorter way, light comes from light—never from the darkness.

Let's apply this to the spiritual struggles we all face every day. What starts with a fleeting thought, if not immediately resisted, progresses into action, which leads to sin, which results in death (James 1:13–15). Don't ever let anyone tell you that temptation is wrong. Temptation isn't wrong; it's normal. If you're not ever tempted, you're already dead! Each temptation of life brings you face-to-face with a moral choice. Either you give in or you stand your ground and say no. Each time you give in—even a little bit—you grow weaker, and each time you resist— even when you resist a small temptation—you grow stronger.

Last summer a dear friend came to see me with news that after many years of struggle she had finally turned the corner in her battle against a debilitating addiction. I told her an illustration that has been very helpful to me. Every day we make hundreds of decisions—most of them very small. We decide what to wear, which way to drive to work, when to go to lunch, which phone call to return first. Many of the decisions we make are either a step into the darkness or a step into the light. I told my friend that each day she would be faced with a thousand tiny decisions, and each one would either lead her back into the darkness or toward the light of life. I also reminded her that she hadn't gotten where she was overnight. It took thousands of tiny decisions to get there, and it would take thousands of tiny decisions to get out. But each day as she took tiny steps toward the light, she would move slowly toward a brand-new life. And I promised her that one day after thousands of tiny steps in the right direction she would wake up surrounded by the light of God on every side.

A few months later she wrote me a wonderful note telling me how marvelously her life has changed in the last ten months. She lives and walks in the light of God's love every day. Bit by bit her life has been transformed. It is nothing short of a miracle. She has discovered the fountain of life, and in His light she has seen the light. Light comes from light—never from the darkness.

*Giver of all light, show me the path that I should take and then give me the strength to take the next step in that direction. Amen.*

— ✳ —

## A MOMENT'S REFLECTION

"Light comes from light." What does that phrase mean? What "small steps toward the light" do you need to take today? Thank God for the progress you have made already.

---
✳
---

# Sixty-Nine

# RESTORING GRACE: HOPE FOR STRAYING SAINTS

*If the Lord delights in a man's way, he makes his steps firm; though he stumble, he will not fall, for the Lord upholds him with his hand.*

Psalm 37:23–24

This week I ate lunch with a man who told me how he came to Christ just a few years ago. He said that after his conversion, someone asked him to explain what it really means to be a Christian. What difference does Jesus make once He becomes both Lord and Savior? His answer was profound: "I've learned that I can sin but I can't enjoy it like I used to." You can still sin, and you can enjoy it for a while, but not forever. God will not let His children enjoy the pleasures of sin indefinitely. Sooner or later, He steps in and brings His wandering sons and daughters back home to Him.

If we graphed the spiritual experience of most Christians, it would move up and down, up and down, up and down—but always moving in a generally upward direction. At any given moment, the graph of your life may show you relatively up or relatively down spiritually. You may be down for a long time, but if you know Jesus, eventually you will start moving up again. I draw two conclusions from this:

1. Direction makes the difference.
2. True believers move toward heaven.

It is possible to fall into grievous sin, but that's not where we belong, and we will not stay there forever. If you are a Christian, you won't be comfortable living in sin. The direction of your life will be away from sin and toward Jesus Christ. It has been said that, "I would rather be one foot away from hell heading toward heaven than one foot away from heaven heading toward hell." Direction makes the difference.

Some people are saved one foot from hell. God turns them around at the very brink of the pit. When they are saved, they still have the smell of brimstone in their clothing. That's why new Christians sometimes look and act pretty rough. They've been snatched from the flames. Some of those same people will still look rough after five or ten years. That's OK because they started so low. You don't judge people by where they are now, but by where they've come from. Take heart in God's restoring grace. The only thing that matters is to keep moving in the right direction.

The direction of the true believer is always ultimately toward heaven. Sometimes we fly like the eagle. Sometimes we run with stallions. Sometimes we walk in victory. And sometimes we're just stumbling upward. I love that phrase—stumbling upward. That's the testimony of nearly all God's saints—we're stumbling upward toward heaven.

> *Father, I praise You for grace so great that it goes beyond my sin, finds me when I have fallen, picks me up, and sets my feet back on the road to heaven. Amen.*

—✳—

## A MOMENT'S REFLECTION

Do you agree that true saints of God will move toward heaven? What is the direction of your life at this moment? Can you think of a time when God's grace restored you when you stumbled?

———— ✳ ————

# Seventy

# SHARED FAITH:
# YOU CAN HELP OTHERS
# GROW STRONGER

*Blessed is he who has regard for the weak; the Lord delivers him in times of trouble.*

Psalm 41:1

The letter was short, to-the-point, and refreshingly honest:

> I felt I should tell you a little bit of a story in hopes it might help someone else. Whenever I tell others about my rough road back to Christ from non-Christian relationships, the one question I am always asked is, "What would have helped make your road back a little easier?" My answer is, during my time of spiritual loneliness, if I had had a sister in Christ seek me out and tell me, "I've been there, I love you, and I can help you find your way back to Jesus," perhaps I could have been spared a lot more pain than having to discover the answers on my own.

She then adds this P.S. "Jesus is never tolerant of sin, but always willing to forgive it. If my experience can help someone else, feel free to use this information."

I certainly am glad to pass it on, because it is truly encouraging. And it reminds us that we will all grow stronger as we lean on each other. If you're having a hard time keeping your head above water, tell someone else. Don't fight the battle all by yourself. Let the Lord minister to you through the resources of the body of Christ.

Check out the verse at the top of this entry. God blesses those who care for the weak. Are you in need of God's blessing right now? Find a brother or sister in need and give him or her a helping hand. So many believers struggle because they try to handle their problems alone. But God never meant that you should walk through the lonely valley by yourself. Hebrews 10:24 says, "Let us consider how we may spur one another on toward love and good deeds." Think of the people you know right now who are going through a hard time. Make a list. Now ask yourself how many others are going through a hard time you don't know about. The truth is, all of us struggle some of the time and some of us struggle most of the time.

When people ask me what they can do to help others, my answer is always the same. Start where you are. Open your eyes to see the hurting faces you meet every day. Our greatest problem is not that we won't help hurting people; it's that all too often we don't even see them in the first place.

Sometimes a positive word can save a life. Desperate people want to know that someone cares about them. Open your eyes. Better yet, ask God to open them for you. Pray for "missionary eyes" to see the needs of those you meet today. You can help someone get better if you will look closely at the faces you see every day.

> *Holy Spirit, give me missionary eyes to see the hurting people all around me. I pray to be a load lifter for a weary pilgrim today. Amen.*

—✳—

## A MOMENT'S REFLECTION

Have you ever felt like the writer of that note, wishing for someone who could help you get back on track? Do you know someone who is in that position right now? What could you do to help the person out?

*Section Eight*
# BUILDING CHARACTER

*The statutes of the Lord are trustworthy,*
*making wise the simple.*

Psalm 19:7

---

❋

# Seventy-One

# CONTENTMENT: HOW GOD WEANS US FROM THE WORLD

*But I have stilled and quieted my soul; like a weaned child with its mother, like a weaned child is my soul within me.*

Psalm 131:2

The picture is one only a mother can fully understand. A child is born and for a long time he looks to his mother's breast as the source of his nourishment. Breakfast, lunch, and supper all come from the same place. When he is hungry, he cries and Mom knows exactly what to do. Her milk satisfies him, and back to sleep he goes.

But the day comes when he has to learn to be satisfied with a bottle. That's not a happy day. He cries, big tears roll down his face, and his arms reach out, but his mother doesn't give in. He fights, he pouts, he screams, all to no avail. What has happened to Mom? She who used to be his friend has now become his enemy. If Mom has a heart at all, she cries too, because from now on things will be different. She will feed him, but never again in the same way.

When the bottle is over, when the tears have stopped, when he learns to eat with his brothers and sisters, then the child comes and lays his head on his mother's breast, not in order to be fed, but just because he loves her. He comes because he wants to be near her.

Here is the truth: Unless a mother weans her child, he will never grow up. He'll be a baby all the days of his life. Though it may seem hard, and though the child misunderstands, if a mother truly loves her child, she will not stop until the job is fully done. When the job is finally done, the child no longer begs for that which it once found indispensable. Once he could not live without his mother's milk; now he no longer needs it.

To be weaned is to have something removed from your life that you thought you couldn't live without. David was saying, "I've come to the place where the things I thought I had to have, I don't need anymore. Now my soul is quiet and content."

Most of us live on the opposite principle. We figure our contentment on the basis of how many of our needs are met. Unfortunately, it's hard to reach a place where all our needs are constantly met. By that standard, it's hard to ever really be content. If contentment is measured by how much of the world's goods you possess, who can ever say, "I have enough"? In our hearts we think, *I would be happy if only I had a new car or a new job or a new dress or a new husband or a new wife.* Since life is hardly ever that simple, we stay frustrated when we ought to be happy.

No wonder we are never satisfied. Instead of being weaned from the world, we are wedded to it. Or maybe I should say, welded to it. In any case, our soul is anything but quiet, our countenance anything but peaceful.

*Lord of my life, wean me from the world that I might draw my nourishment from You alone. Amen.*

———✳———

## A MOMENT'S REFLECTION

Are you a contented person? Is there anything else you need right now to make you truly happy? How has God weaned you from things you once thought you couldn't live without?

## ✴

# Seventy-Two

# WAITING:
# DON'T GIVE UP ON GOD

*In the morning, O Lord, you hear my voice; in the morning
I lay my requests before you and wait in expectation.*

Psalm 5:3

A speaker posed this question to his audience: "If you
could ask God to do one thing for you in the spiritual realm, what would it be?" There is an endless list of
possible answers to a question like that:

- Break a bad habit
- Forgive someone who hurt me
- Have my child come back to God
- See my loved one come to Christ
- Change my character
- Know deliverance from discouragement
- Have new zeal for God
- Receive power to overcome temptation
- Be bold for Christ

Whatever it is, it's not too hard for God.

Each week members of my congregation submit
prayer requests to the staff. Each Tuesday as I look at the
list, I am struck by the many needs of our people. Some

of the requests are truly heartbreaking. Yet as I consider the list, I want to write Genesis 18:14 at the top, "Is anything too hard for the Lord?" No matter how impossible your request may seem to you, it's not too hard for God.

Somewhere I ran across this provocative statement: "The only thing that hinders God is our unbelief." You have to stop and think about that for a moment because it doesn't sound right to say that anything "hinders" God. And in the literal sense, nothing does. He is the Sovereign Lord of the universe. No one can stand against Him. Yet in His wisdom, He has ordained that He will limit His work in the world in accordance with the faith of His people. In that sense, it is perfectly proper to say that our faith or the lack of it either opens the door for the Almighty or "ties His hands," so to speak.

Billy Graham has remarked that heaven is filled with answers for which no one bothered to ask.

Are you willing to wait?

Are you willing to work?

Are you willing to believe God?

What do you believe deep in your heart? Is anything too hard for the Lord? Anything in your life so big that He can't handle it? You already know the answer is no, but I'm asking it in a different way. What problem seems so impossible that part of you doubts that God can take care of it?

God wants us to believe in Him.

He begs us to believe in Him.

He dares us to trust Him.

Is your problem too hard for the Lord? If you answer yes, then there truly is no hope for you. But if you say no, then you have a bright tomorrow!

The choice is yours. Thousands upon thousands of times, many thousands of believers across the centuries have put God to the test. They have trusted Him, and He has come through for them. What about you? Are you willing to trust Him with your problems?

*Eternal God, You are so much bigger than my puny faith. I believe, Lord—help Thou my unbelief. Amen.*

— ✳ —

## A MOMENT'S REFLECTION

Consider the opening question: What one thing would you like God to do for you? Are you willing to wait for Him to work? Write down your request, and then write over it Genesis 18:14.

------ ✳ ------

# Seventy-Three

# TRUST:
# HAVING THE FAITH
# OF A CHILD

*Let the morning bring me word of your unfailing love, for I have put my trust in you. Show me the way I should go, for to you I lift up my soul.*

Psalm 143:8

A few years ago a young woman volunteered to serve as a missionary in Africa. Her young nieces had a hard time understanding why their aunt Rachel would be going so far away. While Rachel was in candidate school in California, Beth (who was only four years old) was talking things over with Rachel's mom. "Grandma, I don't want Rachel to go to Africa."

"But Rachel has to go. God called her and said, 'Rachel, I want you to go to Africa.'"

Beth thought about that for a moment. Then she said, "How do we know He was talking about our Rachel? He might have meant some other Rachel." Then, summoning up all her reasoning powers, she asked a crucial question: "Did He use her first name and her last name?" Did He just say, "Rachel" or did He specify, "Rachel Jones"? After all, there are a lot of Rachels in the world, and He could have meant someone else. The grandmother decided that this was such an important question that she and Beth called Rachel in California. Rachel told Beth that God had indeed used her first name and her last name. Thus reassured, four-year-old Beth gave her blessing for Aunt Rachel to go to the mission field.

That, I think, is what Jesus meant when He said, "Unless you change and become like little children, you will never enter the kingdom of heaven" (Matthew 18:3). The faith that pleases God is childlike in its simplicity.

The word for "trust" in Hebrew means "to lean with the full body," "to lay upon," "to rest the full weight upon." In our thinking, the word trust means to rely upon or to have confidence in. But the Hebrew word is stronger. It is the idea of stretching yourself out upon a bed or resting on a hard surface. To trust in the Lord is to rest your whole weight upon Him.

Trusting God isn't easy for many people. I'm thinking now of friends who moved from Chicago to a distant city. As the time drew near, the emotional stress of leaving the familiar for the unknown almost overwhelmed the wife. I think she would probably say that making this particular move was the single most difficult thing she has ever had to do. Just before leaving, she made an interesting comment: "How did we get here? In my heart I believe we're doing the right thing, but looking back I'm not sure how we got from Point A to Point B. Only God could have done it, because I never would have done it myself." But she smiled when she said it.

Trusting God often involves great uncertainty and periods of deep doubt. But if you are willing to do what He wants you to do, He then takes responsibility to reach into the chaos of life and lead you step-by-step to the place He wants you to be.

*Lord God, thank You for stepping into the confusion of my life and leading me forward. I still need Your help today. Amen.*

——✳——

## A MOMENT'S REFLECTION

What does the phrase "childlike faith" mean to you? Do you find it hard to trust God right now? Are you currently at "Point A" or "Point B" or somewhere in between?

*

# Seventy-Four

# MEEKNESS: YOUR POWER UNDER GOD'S CONTROL

*But the meek will inherit the land and enjoy great peace.*
Psalm 37:11

The word meek does not have a positive connotation in our culture. It suggests many things, none of which are very appealing. If you tell someone you think he is meek, he will probably not take it as a compliment. In fact, he will probably think you are implying something negative about his character.

A quick check of the thesaurus bears this out. Here are some listed synonyms for "meek": humble, docile, mild, calm, gentle, peaceful, tame, submissive, soft, spineless, passive, and broken. Some of those words are positive; others are not. Another source lists the following phrases as illustrative of meekness: "to eat dirt," "to lick the dust," "to cringe like a dog," "to take it on the chin."

That graphically illustrates the problem. Just try sticking some of those words and phrases in the third beatitude (Matthew 5:5) and see what you get:

"Blessed are the spineless, for they will inherit the earth." It doesn't sound right, does it?

Or how about, "Blessed are those who cringe like a dog." It's hard to imagine Jesus (or anyone else) saying that.

It's no wonder that we don't want to be called meek. I wouldn't either, if that's what the word really means. None of us likes to be bullied. We'd all rather be loved. We tend to value tough, strong, assertive leaders.

The biblical concept of meekness means having your power under God's control. During a radio interview I was asked to explain meekness as it applies to being a Christian man in today's world. That was not the first time I've been asked that question. I think many men would not feel complimented if someone called them "meek." Yet the interviewer pointed out that Jesus used that very word to describe Himself in Matthew 11:29 (KJV). It seems to me that if Jesus felt comfortable calling Himself "meek" (or "gentle" in some translations, including the NIV), we shouldn't have a big problem with it.

And after all, Jesus was no pushover. The same Jesus who embraced the children also took a whip and cleaned out the temple. Say what you will about it, but don't call Him a sissy. When He confronted sin, He was gentle like a tornado is gentle. But when the moment called for it, He could be tender and forgiving.

Gentleness is not weakness. It is our power under God's control. It is the ability to give of ourselves to help the hurting while at the same time confronting evil whenever necessary. That's a tough combination, but our Lord pulled it off without a hitch.

*Holy Spirit, make me like Jesus that my power might be fully under God's control. Amen.*

— ✳ —

## A MOMENT'S REFLECTION

When you think of the word meek, what images come to mind? Is your power under your control, under God's control, or out of control? Would your friends use the word meek to describe you?

---
✳
---

# Seventy-Five

# HEALING:
# IT STARTS IN YOUR HEART

*Be merciful to me, Lord, for I am faint; O Lord, heal me,*
*for my bones are in agony.*

Psalm 6:2

Psalm 6 is commonly called the first of the penitential psalms—those that express a sense of personal sin and a cry to God for help. The precise circumstances behind David's prayer are not known, and perhaps do not matter, because they speak to a universal need—the need for forgiveness and healing of the mind, body, and soul.

Doctors have known for a long time that there is a close relationship between the physical and the spiritual sides of life. Even though the precise relationship is difficult to define or to quantify, every doctor has seen the principle in action. Ask any doctor and he or she will tell stories about patients who should have died but didn't—the only possible explanation was their positive, hope-filled outlook on life. Ask that same doctor and he or she will give you other stories of people who came into treatment in a negative or angry or hostile mode and who stayed sick longer than they should have. And every doctor has seen patients die when they should have gotten better.

When you approach life positively and with an optimistic outlook, you are much more likely to stay healthy. A negative attitude seems to go along with poor health. Solomon reflected this truth when he wrote that "a cheerful heart is good medicine, but a crushed spirit dries up the bones" (Proverbs 17:22).

I also find it fascinating that James connected prayer for healing with confession of sin (James 5:14–16). He seemed to imply that when the elders pray over the sick, they are to inquire as to the spiritual status of the sick person, which suggests that the sickness might be connected with unresolved issues in the soul.

Over the twenty years of my ministry I have seen this principle over and over again. As the leaders of the church gather to pray for the sick, we always ask, "Are you aware of anything in your life that might be causing your current sickness?" Usually the answer is negative, but occasionally the person will respond with a confession that involves bitterness, unforgiveness, or other debilitating sins that can block God's healing power.

This is not to suggest that all sickness is connected to personal sin. Sometimes it is, and when that happens, thoughtful Christians will encourage the person to take steps of confession, repentance, and (where appropriate) restitution. In other cases, sickness exists not because of any particular sin but simply as a result of living in a sin-cursed world.

When Jesus comes back, sin and sickness will finally be banished from the earth forever. Until that day, believers have the opportunity to demonstrate their faith in the midst of sickness, and we also have the privilege of bringing our cases to the Great Physician and asking for the healing we need.

*Lord Jesus, create in me a clean heart that I might be healed from the inside out. Amen.*

— ✳ —

## A MOMENT'S REFLECTION

Do you agree that a person's spiritual state plays a crucial role in the healing process? Have you ever seen anyone get better (or worse) because of this principle? Why does healing almost always begin in the heart?

---

# Seventy-Six

# BIBLICAL OPTIMISM: LOOKING FORWARD TO THE FUTURE

*I am still confident of this: I will see the goodness of the Lord in the land of the living.*

Psalm 27:13

Biblical optimism is based on the gospel of Jesus Christ and not on your circumstances. That's a crucial principle to grasp. You may be facing difficult circumstances right now, and your tendency might be to think, *Psalm 27:13 doesn't apply to me.* You may be going through a tough time financially, and you think, *Nothing could ever change this.* Or your marriage may be in trouble and divorce may seem the only option. You may be on the verge of losing your job. Or your health. Or a dream you've pursued for many years. There may be trouble in your family or at school or on the job. And as you survey the situation, you can't find any grounds for encouragement.

That doesn't matter. It is still possible to be optimistic, because biblical optimism rests on the promises of the Gospel and not on your circumstances. As long as the Gospel is true (and it is), great change is possible, even in apparently hopeless situations.

That perspective changes the way we look at disappointment and discouragement. If God's number one goal is to make me like Jesus Christ (see Romans 8:28–29), then He has many lessons to teach me. Most of those lessons can only come through heartache and difficulty, because most of us learn more through the hard times than we do through the good times.

God's work in your life is a process of chipping away at your weak points and slowly developing the character of Jesus Christ within. But that means there are tremendous grounds for optimism—even in the worst situations—because the hard times mean that God is hard at work in you to make you more like His Son.

Nothing is wasted. Nothing that happens to you is meant to destroy you. Even the attacks and slanders of your enemies are allowed by God for a higher purpose in your life. Everything has a purpose in your life. Everything. The fact that you don't always see it doesn't negate that fact.

So be encouraged. God is at work in your life, especially in the hard times.

*Lord of my life, give me long-range vision to see that even my difficulties have a purpose in Your eternal plan. Amen.*

---*---

## A MOMENT'S REFLECTION

Are you a biblical optimist? Name three places you have seen "the goodness of the Lord" in your own life in the last week. Name several areas of your life that are still "under construction" by God.

Seventy-Seven

# GOSSIP: STEALING SOMEONE'S GOOD NAME

*All my enemies whisper together against me; they imagine the worst for me.*

Psalm 41:7

Here is a thief who lives inside most churches. He (or she) is a thief because he steals the good name of someone else. "Psssst . . . Have you heard the latest?" "Did you know that Sally and Bill are splitting up?" "She never intended to pay the money back." "He said he was sick but I'll bet he was just playing golf." "I'm glad she lost her job. She needed to get some humility." "Those Johnson kids are the worst children in church. I think the middle one will probably end up in Congress . . . or in jail . . . or both."

On and on it goes. In politics the level of public discourse has reached an all-time low. We seem fixated on the salacious details of the private lives of our leaders. Each candidate perfects his sleazy attack ads on the opposition, carefully twisting the facts, slightly distorting the truth, until a negative image is drawn. We say we don't like it, but politicians wouldn't use those ads if we didn't pay attention to them.

No church is immune to the problem of gossip, including the church where I am the pastor. People love to talk, and they love to talk about other people. This is an undeniable fact of human nature. How do you know when you've "crossed the line" from conversation to gossip? When truth is sacrificed, you've crossed the line. But you can tell the truth and still gossip if your intent is to make another person look bad.

Just remember this. When you gossip about other people, you're guilty of stealing their good name. You are guilty of robbery just as much as the mugger who holds you up on the street. And you aren't any less guilty in God's eyes. No, you are worse because you do it in God's house and you attack God's children.

Shakespeare said it well in these famous words from Othello:

Who steals my purse, steals trash; 'tis something, nothing;
'Twas mine, 'tis his, and has been slave to thousands;
But he that filches from me my good name
Robs me of that which not enriches him,
And makes me poor indeed.

If any other evidence needs to be mentioned, remember that gossip is listed in Romans 1:29–31—along with murder—as one mark of a depraved life. There is such a thing as a gossiping thief—a category that may apply to you more than you think.

Here's a test. Just go to three close friends this week

and ask them: Do you think I have a tendency to gossip?
You might be surprised at the answers you get.

*O Lord, may my words be used only to build up and
never to tear down. Amen.*

———— ✳ ————

## A MOMENT'S REFLECTION

What is the essential difference between talking about
others and harmful gossip? Have you ever been harmed
by the gossiping words of others? Ask God to create a
sensitivity in your heart so that you will think twice before you gossip about others.

---
✳
---

# Seventy-Eight

# GRACIOUS LIPS: THE POWER OF KIND WORDS

*Even in darkness light dawns for the upright, for the gracious and compassionate and righteous man.*

Psalm 112:4

One of my seminary professors liked to remind us that "it takes no size to criticize." I often think about that when I am tempted to take cheap shots at other people. The world is filled with critics; where are the affirmers? On every hand we have self-appointed "truth-tellers" whose calling in life seems to be finding what's wrong with everyone else. You know if you listen to them long enough they'll soon begin sniping at others.

But there is a better way. Years ago I picked up a copy of the Four-Way Test. It consists of four questions to ask yourself when you are tempted to say something unkind.

1. Is it the truth?
2. Is it fair to all concerned?
3. Will it build goodwill and better friendships?
4. Will it be beneficial to all concerned?

Pretty simple, isn't it? What a difference it would make if we would apply those four questions this week.

Proverbs 18:21 says, "The tongue has the power of life and death." Think about that. Every time you open your mouth either life or death comes out. What has been coming out of your mouth this week? Life or death?

Some people can't keep friends because they speak death into every relationship. They are so critical and petty that they kill every friendship they have. Many marriages die because we kill them with our unkind words. Some families fall apart because the parents kill their children with harsh words. The same can be true where we work. We destroy our team spirit through backbiting, gossip, slander, and lying.

What do these things bring to a relationship?

- Death in our lips
- A corpse in our mouth
- The stench of the grave in our words

But the other side is also true. We may give life by the things we say.

- Positive words
- Hopeful comments
- Life-giving affirmations
- Kind expressions

Here is the bottom line. When we affirm others, God affirms them through us and His name is honored. As one writer put it, "God becomes believable as we become lovable." We know this is not a fanciful connection since the last phrase of Psalm 112:4 is applied to God in Psalm 111:4. As Spurgeon pointed out, when God makes a man upright, He makes him like Himself. As we open our lips to speak words of kindness, the Spirit of Christ goes with our words and uses them to point men and women to God.

*May my lips, O Lord, be the very lips of Jesus—filled with grace and truth. Amen.*

— ✳ —

## A MOMENT'S REFLECTION

Are you a critic—or an affirmer? How much "death" has come out of your mouth in the last three days? Pray that God would help you speak life into every situation you encounter today.

❋

# Seventy-Nine

# HAPPINESS: CURING THE "IF ONLYS" OF LIFE

*But may the righteous be glad and rejoice before God; may they be happy and joyful.*

Psalm 68:3

Are you happy? Really happy? Are you satisfied with your life? Here is the startling truth: If things could make us happy, we'd be in paradise every day. We think "more is better." Is it? It seems the more we have, the less we like it.

Perhaps you've heard the story about the king who fell into a serious depression. Nothing could lift his spirits. His servants tried everything—music, dancing, court jesters, lavish banquets, beautiful flowers—yet nothing seemed to help him. Finally an old and wise man came to the king with an unusual piece of advice. "O King, if you can obtain the shirt off the back of a truly happy man, you yourself will be happy." Upon hearing those words, the king ordered his men to search the four corners of the earth and bring him the shirt off the back of a truly happy man. Weeks passed, then months. Finally his soldiers returned. "O King, after many days and much searching, we found a truly happy man. But your majesty, the man was not wearing a shirt."

How fitting, how true to life. We think to ourselves, "If only I had . . ." and then we fill in the blank with our latest dream. A new house, a new wife, a new set of children, a new job, a new school, a new career, a new church, a new portfolio, a new start in life.

Oh, how happy we'd be . . . if only! No wonder we're unhappy. No wonder we're discontented. No wonder we're miserable. No wonder we dream so much. Coveting has done its evil work within. It has bored its way into our soul, eating away our happiness, leaving us empty, frustrated, and angry.

But that raises a question. At what point does legitimate desire become coveting? Coveting occurs either when I desire something I have no right to have (e.g., my neighbor's wife) or when the desire becomes the controlling passion of my life so that I begin to believe that my happiness depends on the acquisition of the item itself.

- A new house may be nice, but my happiness does not depend on a new house. If it does, then I am coveting.
- A new car may help me get around, but it can't be the source of my happiness. If it is, then I am coveting.

The moment I trick myself into thinking, *This [item or goal] is necessary for my happiness in life,* then I have crossed the line into coveting.

David reminds us in Psalm 68:3 of a truth we already

know—but often forget. Happy are they who find their happiness in God. They shall be happy indeed.

*Lord, do whatever it takes to make me happy in You. If that means making me miserable with the things of this world, so be it. Amen.*

———✳———

## A MOMENT'S REFLECTION

How happy are you right now? What else do you need in order to be happy at this moment? What does it mean to you to find happiness in God?

*Eighty*

———————— ✳ ————————

# SLOW DOWN!
# TAKING TIME TO
# HEAR HIS VOICE

*My soul yearns, even faints, for the courts of the Lord; my heart and my flesh cry out for the living God.*

Psalm 84:2

This week I had a chance to stop and worship God in an extended way for the first time in seven years. I spent four days with seventy-five other pastors in a Pastor's Prayer Summit. In my years as a pastor I've been to many camps, conferences, and retreats, but never have I been to anything like a Prayer Summit. For four days—from Monday afternoon until Thursday noon—we met together with no agenda but worshiping God. There were no sermons, no bulletins, and no set program. We simply gathered in a large circle and waited for God to speak to us. Sometimes we sang together, sometimes we bowed in silent prayer, often we prayed together. On Tuesday the leaders put a chair in the middle of the circle and offered pastors a chance to ask for prayer for their personal needs. I saw pastors weeping over their sins and grown men embracing each other with words of healing and forgiveness.

It was an awesome experience for me personally. But as I look back, I realize that I was so wound up when I got there that it took me two days to relax enough to enjoy it. And about the time I started getting in the swing of things, it was time to go home.

On our last night there, someone spontaneously prayed, "Lord, wouldn't it be great if what happened here could happen every day to every man when we go back home." It would be great, wouldn't it? Why can't we experience God's presence every day? Whatever answer you give to that question, just remember that God is not the problem. He's always ready to meet you any time of the day or night.

Does your heart cry out for the living God? Do you yearn for the courts of the Lord? Or have the demands of a busy schedule and the reality of overcommitment stifled your desire for the Lord?

As with so many other areas of life, the problem is within us. We're too busy to hear God's voice. We're running so hard and so fast that God would have to shout to get our attention. Sometimes that's what He does. He shouts through pain or opposition or sickness or disappointment, and suddenly we begin to hear His voice.

It doesn't have to be that way. God always speaks loud enough for a listening ear to hear.

*Slow me down, Lord, so that I can once again hear Your still, small voice. Amen.*

— ✷ —

## A MOMENT'S REFLECTION

How long has been it since you slowed down for more than a few minutes? What happens to people who run in "high gear" all the time? How can you alter your schedule to include more time to listen to God's voice?

Section Nine
# CRUCIAL CHOICES

*If my people would but listen to me, if Israel would follow my ways, how quickly would I subdue their enemies and turn my hand against their foes!*

Psalm 81:13–14

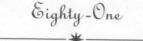

# Eighty-One

# A QUIET TIME: DAILY TIME WITH THE LORD

*Open my eyes that I may see wonderful things in your law.*
Psalm 119:18

I first learned this verse more than a quarter century ago when a Christian college professor used it as his theme verse for our course in Old Testament Survey. Dr. Wymal Porter encouraged us to make this verse our prayer as we studied the fascinating history of God's dealings with Israel. Ever since then it has reminded me that I must pray for God's illumination, for without it I am just reading words on paper.

This verse also reminds us that there is power in the Word of God when its divine authority is accepted in a believing heart. The Word is energized within us as we believe it. It is like farmland that bears a rich harvest. It is like a gold mine that delivers great riches. It is like an investment that pays a huge dividend. When our eyes are opened to see the "wonderful things" in God's Word, it comes alive within us and produces a bountiful harvest.

The summer after learning this verse, I served as a counselor at Word of Life Island in Schroon Lake, New York, where I was exposed for the first time to a concept called "the quiet time." A quiet time means that you set aside a few minutes each day to read the Bible and pray. The people at Word of Life were so committed to it that they set aside thirty minutes every day when the whole camp stopped and we all went off and had a quiet time. We even had a little diary that we filled in with our thoughts and prayers.

Some people would call it devotions, others the morning watch. It makes no difference what title you use. In the years since then I have read hundreds of books on the spiritual life. When all is said and done, I know of nothing more important for maintaining a warm relationship with Jesus Christ than this—a consistent, regular, quality quiet time.

It has not gotten easier over the years. In many ways it has gotten harder. It almost always does, because we tend to substitute our knowledge and Christian activity for this simple discipline of a daily time with God and His Word.

I commend to you the practice of a daily quiet time. How can we say we believe the Bible and accept its authority if we do not daily spend time in the Word? If you are an elder or a deacon or a deaconess, if you attend a Christian college or if you work for a Christian organization, if you have been a Christian for many years, if you teach Sunday school or serve the Lord in some way, I exhort you not to rationalize that your knowledge makes a quiet time unnecessary. New Christians rarely have to be convinced about this. Experienced Christians often forget this truth and suffer spiritually as a result.

*Eternal Father, let Your Word be planted deep in my heart today that it may bring forth a harvest of righteousness in my life. Amen.*

—✳—

## A MOMENT'S REFLECTION

Do you agree that a daily time with the Lord is important for your spiritual growth? How consistent are you in this area? Memorize Psalm 119:18 and then share it with a friend.

# Eighty-Two

# FRIENDS: CHOOSE WISELY OR WISH YOU HAD

*I do not sit with deceitful men, nor do I consort with hypocrites.*
Psalm 26:4

The e-mail message told a sad but not unfamiliar story:

> I don't think you would expect a message from me, but I felt God directing me to write you. It is kind of hard to find my words and I feel a bit awkward, but here it goes anyway. Jesus spoke to my heart tonight and it has been quite awhile since I've listened. I have ignored His calling for a couple of years now. It is truly amazing the way I was taken off guard.

> Years ago I accepted Christ into my heart. At first I wanted to do His will and live a Christian life. I have slipped quite a bit since then. I wanted to experience all that I was told not to do and I did. I thought I was happy, but inside I was crying out for help. I latched on to a group of friends that weren't exactly following the right path. The friendship quickly died. Then I joined another group of friends that had an even worse effect on my life. I thought they were true

friends and again Christ disagreed (I didn't realize it till now though). I was stuck pretty much friendless this year, living on my own. I couldn't understand what was wrong with my personality and why it was so hard to keep friends. I now understand that God had a plan to destroy those dangerous relationships.

I asked God to take me back tonight and have not stopped crying since. I guess I am asking you to pray for me because I don't want to lose this desire. I want to change and do God's will. I know true happiness comes from seeing Jesus and I want a clear picture. It is so hard to be alone, but if I put Christ first He will be all I need.

As I reflect on that letter, it occurs to me that it might have been written by many people I know. Change a detail here or there and it might be one of a hundred personal stories. It speaks to the awesome power of relationships for good or for evil. Many Christians don't understand that no relationship stays static. Relationships are like rivers that continually flow this way or that. Every friendship either pulls us up toward God or drags us down toward hell.

The apostle Paul understood both sides of this truth. In 1 Corinthians 15:33 he wrote that "bad company corrupts good character." Eventually we all become like the people we spend time with. For better or worse, we become like our friends—whether we like it or not.

*Lord Jesus, I pray for the discernment to choose friends who will bring me closer to You. Amen.*

—— ✳ ——

## A MOMENT'S REFLECTION

Think about your five closest friends. What spiritual impact have they had on your life? And what impact have you had on them? Do you need to make some changes in this area?

---
＊
---

# Eighty-Three

# GENEROUS GIVING: A SIGN OF GOD'S GRACE AT WORK

*I was young and now I am old, yet I have never seen the righteous forsaken or their children begging bread. They are always generous and lend freely; their children will be blessed.*

Psalm 37:25–26

Here is an amazing truth. God promises to bless generous givers. He even promises to bless their children. That's reason enough to give until the day you die. Most of us have a bit of built-in selfishness as part of our basic nature. In a day of high prices, unemployment, and much uncertainty, it's easy to focus all your energy on building up your net worth and to forget about people.

When you give money to a worthy cause, when you cook a meal for a friend, when you give a bag of groceries, when you anonymously slip a twenty-dollar bill in an envelope and mail it, when you move to meet the real needs around you, you are doing exactly what God expects—you are supplying the needs of the saints.

I've never forgotten something that happened when I pastored a small church in the Los Angeles area many years ago. One young couple in that church experienced a long string of setbacks: unemployment, sickness, losing their home, family problems of every description. At one point the wife became pregnant and was expecting twins. Late in the pregnancy, complications developed and one of the babies died before delivery. At that moment, the husband got sick and couldn't work. The roof caved in around them. The church rallied to their cause, raised money on their behalf, bought groceries, prepared meals, and helped pay the rent. Church members helped take care of the children and did the chores around the house until the family could get on their feet. Sometime later, after the crisis had passed, the wife sent the church a note that said something like this: "I thank God for all you have done. God used you to help us out when we really needed help. I'm glad to be part of a church that cares."

Our giving not only meets physical needs, it also causes a great chorus of thanksgiving to rise up before the throne of God. When we give to help others, they know we do it in the name of Jesus of Nazareth who went about doing good—and they glorify God who made our giving possible.

How does it work? When we give as Christians, there is a divine nametag attached to every dollar we give, every meal we cook, and every piece of clothing we donate. Our giving reflects on our heavenly Father and enhances His reputation in the world.

*O Father, You have given me all that I possess. I pray now to be given the gift of a generous spirit. Amen.*

—✳—

## A MOMENT'S REFLECTION

Can you think of a time when you were on the receiving end of generous giving by other Christians? What did you learn from that experience? Would the people who know you best call you a generous person?

———— ✳ ————

# Eighty-Four

# PRIORITIES: INVESTING IN YOUR OWN FUTURE

*You have made known to me the path of life; you will fill me with joy in your presence, with eternal pleasures at your right hand.*

Psalm 16:11

A motivational speaker begins every talk with this penetrating question: "Do you know why God put you where you are right now?" That's a tough question for some of us to answer. Have you wondered about that? Why has God put you where you are right now? Do you think it happened by chance that you are single (or married), with children at home (or long since moved away), with a good job (or stuck in a bad situation)? Or is there a larger purpose at work in your life?

Let me ask that question from a completely different perspective: What will you have to show for your life when you stand before Jesus Christ?

A good job?
A college degree?
Money in the bank?
Lots of friends?

A large reputation?
A successful career?
The praise of others?

If that's all you've got to show for your life, then you really don't have much going for you. Sooner than you think, you'll be lying in a box six feet underground with grass growing over your head, and all the things of this life won't matter at all. Someone else will have your money and your job. Your fame will fade, your glory will disappear, and everything you now own will belong to others. You yourself will eventually be forgotten except by those people who stumble on your gravestone a hundred years from now and say, "I wonder who this guy was."

Howard Hendricks said it this way: "Only two things in this world are eternal—the Word of God and people. It only makes sense to build your life around those things that will last forever." The Word of God will last forever. People last forever. Everything else disappears.

When asked by a job interviewer about his goal in life, one man responded: "My goal in life is to go to heaven and to take as many people with me as possible." That's a thoroughly biblical worldview.

Some years ago I heard Dr. Vernon Grounds say that whenever we are faced with a major decision, we ought to ask ourselves, "What difference will this make in ten thousand years?" Most of the things we worry so much about won't matter in three weeks, let alone three months or three years. We focus on the trivial and forget to pursue the eternal. But ten thousand times ten thousand years from now, you'll still be glad you invested your life for Jesus Christ.

*Lord of all things, help me to invest now in those things that will pay eternal dividends. Amen.*

—✳—

## A MOMENT'S REFLECTION

Go back through this entry and answer each question. Why do you think God put you where you are right now? As you think about the things you have done in the last week, which ones won't matter in ten thousand years?

※

# Eighty-Five

# CHOICES: STAYING CLEAN IN A DIRTY WORLD

*How can a young man keep his way pure? By living according to your word.*

Psalm 119:9

When I was a student in a Christian college many years ago, Lehman Strauss spoke at one of our Bible conferences. One day he gave a message on the topic of purity. I have forgotten everything about that message except for one illustration. He commented that some years earlier he had begun making a list of the men he had known in the ministry who had fallen through sexual sin. I think he said the list had reached to more than seventy names. But recently, he said, he had heard about another good friend who had fallen. It broke his heart to the point that he tore up the list and threw it away.

I am not exempt from this temptation. Neither are you. Let me give some practical guidelines for dealing with sexual temptation.

1. Don't rely on your own strength; know your limits.
2. Stay out of questionable areas.
3. Don't fight the battle alone.

4. Don't make excuses.
5. Be honest about your problem.
6. Trace the cycle of lust in your life.
7. Remember who you are.

That last point is critical. You have a father and a mother, and you probably have brothers and sisters. You probably have a husband or wife and children. You certainly have friends who love you. You've got people at work or at school who depend on you. You've even got casual acquaintances who watch you and unbelievers who know you are a Christian. Put simply, you can't afford to let all those people down and to be shamed in front of them.

Above and beyond all that, remember who you are in Christ. You are a child of God, a totally new creation. You are saved, redeemed, justified, forgiven, regenerated, and seated with Christ in heavenly places. All the promises of God now belong to you. You bear the name of your heavenly Father. You are called to live to His glory. You were made for better things. You were not made to live in sin.

First Thessalonians 4:8 reminds us that it is "God who gives you his Holy Spirit." The word "gives" is present tense. In this case it means that God gives and keeps on giving the Spirit to you. You have the Holy Spirit always within you. Therefore, when God commands you to abstain, He also gives you the power to obey.

What a wonderful thought. You are not in this battle alone! Your weakness is His strength. Do you need help? You've got it.

283

There is no power but this to sanctify you. There is no hope but this for cleansing from sin.

How can you please God? What is His will for your life? God's Word offers many answers to those questions. One that is absolutely clear is this: You are to abstain from sexual immorality. That is always part of His will for your life.

*Spirit of the Living God, cleanse me from the inside out so that my passion becomes a pure stream and not a polluted river. Amen.*

———✳———

A MOMENT'S REFLECTION

Make a list of the people who are depending on you to make wise choices. What is the best argument you know for staying morally pure? Review the seven steps and apply them to your own life.

—————— ✳ ——————

# Eighty-Six

# PLEASING GOD: MAKE IT YOUR ULTIMATE GOAL

*May the words of my mouth and the meditation of my heart be pleasing in your sight, O Lord, my Rock and my Redeemer.*
Psalm 19:14

The closing verse of Psalm 19 teaches us what we already know—that we need God's help so that our words and thoughts might please Him. In the preceding two verses David cried out to God for cleansing from "hidden faults" and "willful sins." Sometimes we sin and don't even know it; other times we sin openly. Both cases desperately need God's forgiveness that we might be "blameless" in His eyes (v. 13).

It is not wrong to receive praise from men, especially for a job well done. Good work ought to be praised. However, it's wrong to do your work solely—or even mostly—for the purpose of receiving the praise of man. We don't need spiritual groupies or some kind of spiritual PR Department that will make us feel better about ourselves. What we want and what we seek is the praise of almighty God.

If we seek the praise of others, we shall have it—and that is all we shall have. Pleasing God is something else entirely. Let's set up a comparison of those two ideas for just a moment.

People Pleaser:
- Refuses to speak hard truth
- Says what people want to hear
- Flip-flops on crucial issues
- Says one thing to one person; another to another
- Obedient when convenient
- Tells the truth most of the time
- Unwilling to offend over issues of truth

God Pleaser:
- Willing to speak all the truth
- Says what people need to hear
- Consistent at all times
- Says the same thing all the time
- Obedient even when it hurts
- Tells the truth all the time
- Willing to offend in order to be faithful to God

Let us suppose that you have been feeling sick lately. When you go to the doctor, he administers a test. The results are not good. The outlook is grim, but the disease is treatable if you get started now. What do you want the doctor to do? If he tells you the truth, you'll be devastated. If he doesn't, you'll be dead. Would you rather have him sugarcoat the truth or even lie to you? Or do you want to know the whole truth about your condition? I know the answer for me. When I go to the doctor, I want to know the whole truth even if it hurts. But what if he says, "I want to spare you pain"? "Doc, tell that to my wife and children at my funeral," I reply.

When life-and-death issues are at stake, only the truth will do. When it comes to the gospel of Jesus Christ, the stakes couldn't be higher. Therefore, Christians must be people who hold to the highest possible standards of truth and integrity. There is no other way to please God.

*Lord Jesus, raise me above the smiles and frowns of this world so that my only concern will be Your approval. Amen.*

— * —

## A MOMENT'S REFLECTION

Are you a people pleaser or a God pleaser? What would your friends say about you? Why is truth telling an important part of pleasing God?

---
✳
---

# Eighty-Seven

# FEAR OF THE LORD: WHERE WISDOM BEGINS

*The fear of the Lord is the beginning of wisdom; all who follow his precepts have good understanding.*

Psalm 111:10

The "fear of the Lord" is a major biblical theme in both testaments. It is the key to long life, wisdom, prosperity, knowledge, and happiness. It is the single most important quality a father can hand down to his children.

Two other Old Testament verses clarify what it is: (1) It is an attitude of the heart. "Oh, that their hearts would be inclined to fear me and keep all my commands always, so that it might go well with them and their children forever!" (Deuteronomy 5:29). (2) It is a choice. "They hated knowledge and did not choose to fear the Lord" (Proverbs 1:29).

What is the fear of the Lord? It is the personal choice of respectful love that makes you want to do the things that please Him. It is not cringing fear. That's respect without love. It's also not irreverent flippancy. That can be love without respect.

The fear of the Lord is not the opposite of love. It's what real love is all about. It is the basis of a healthy relationship with God. When I choose to fear the Lord, I am choosing out of respect and love to do the things that please Him. All that I do in my life comes back to this.

Fearing God means taking Him seriously. That's why the fear of the Lord is where holiness begins. In a world where most people take God lightly, anyone who takes God seriously will stand out as different, separate, distinct. That's what the word holy means.

What are the marks of those who take God seriously? They avoid evil, have a tender conscience, are eager to know what pleases God, and guard against temptation.

This answers so many questions: What made the saints of old stand strong in the face of persecution, suffering, and torture? They feared God more than they feared man. What makes single mothers keep bringing their children to church week after week? They take God seriously. What makes a businessman refuse a promotion that would take him away from his family and his church? He takes God seriously. What gives teenagers the courage to just say no? They take God seriously. What makes a woman give up a lucrative career as a surgeon to serve God in Nigeria? She takes God seriously. What makes a young couple decide to become foster parents? They take God seriously. What is it that makes a fellow get up early to read the Bible and pray? Nothing more than this: He takes God seriously. Why do some Christians keep praying year after year for others to be saved? Because they take God seriously. Why do parents dedicate their children in front of the congregation? Because they take God seriously.

Here is the truth in one sentence: Holy living is

motivated by a godly fear that does not take lightly what was purchased at so great a cost.

*Holy Father, I pray that my life may show that godly fear and great joy spring from the same eternal fountain. Amen.*

——✸——

## A MOMENT'S REFLECTION

Define in practical terms what it means to "fear the Lord." Would a person watching your life conclude that you take God seriously? Why is the fear of the Lord the "beginning" of wisdom?

---
✳
---

# Eighty-Eight

# FACING THE TRUTH:
# IT WILL HURT YOU FIRST

*Surely you desire truth in the inner parts; you teach me wisdom in the inmost place.*

Psalm 51:6

Some years ago I visited a gifted counselor who gave me a personality inventory and later mailed me the results. Enclosed with the test results were some sheets of paper the counselor had written. On one page the counselor had done a takeoff on the famous words of Jesus, "You will know the truth, and the truth will set you free" (John 8:32) He had taken the last phrase and printed it like this: "The truth shall make you free . . . but it will hurt you first."

It startled me, and then it was as if someone had turned on a light above my head. Yes, of course, it makes perfect sense. The truth will set you free but it will hurt you first. In a flash I realized why most people have trouble growing spiritually. It's not because we don't know the truth. We've got so much truth it's running out our eyeballs. We hear the truth at church, on the radio, from our friends, from books and tapes and seminars and concerts. And we get it straight from the Bible. That's not our problem. If just knowing the truth were all we needed, we'd all be candidates for perfection in this life.

No, the problem runs deeper than that. We know the truth, but we don't want to let it hurt us, so we deflect it, ignore it, deny it, attack it, argue with it, and in general avoid it in any way we can. We put up a shield of defenses so we can deflect the incoming bullets of truth. After a while we get so good at deflection that the truth never gets through to us at all.

Therefore, we are not set free. We're still angry . . . stubborn . . . bitter . . . greedy . . . arrogant . . . filled with lust . . . self-willed . . . critical . . . and unkind.

When David cried out for God's mercy, he acknowledged the true source of the problem—and where the healing must begin. Until there is "truth" (the word means something like "reality" as opposed to making excuses, covering up, and pretending everything is OK) in the inner recesses of the soul, healing can never begin. As long as we lie to ourselves, we can never get better, and God cannot teach wisdom in the inmost place. Would you like to be set free? You'll have to let the truth hurt you first.

*Lord God, give me the courage to face the truth about myself so that I can be set free. Amen.*

— ✳ —

## A MOMENT'S REFLECTION

Why is knowing the truth never enough to produce spiritual growth? Name some ways people hide from painful truth. In what areas of your life are you lying to yourself (or making silly excuses)?

---
✳
---

# Eighty-Nine

# WORRY:
# THE FRUIT OF A
# DIVIDED HEART

*When anxiety was great within me, your consolation brought joy to my soul.*

Psalm 94:19

The word anxiety comes from a root that means "to divide." That's because anxiety produces a divided mind, one which is pulled this way and that way, constantly distracted and disturbed. Here's the point: Either the Lord carries the worry or we do. If we do, we'll be divided, distracted, disturbed. And we will end up confused, frustrated, and burdened. If He carries the load, we may still have trouble and difficulties, but no anxiety, no dominating fear, no undue concern, no hopeless despair.

There's a reason we can do that with confidence—"your consolation brought joy to my soul." This touches a secret fear of many believers—that if we submit our lives to Jesus Christ, He'll mess things up. He'll ask us to do things we don't want to do, He'll send us places we don't want to go, He'll bring unpleasant people into our lives and force us to be someone we don't want to be. And we secretly fear He can't be trusted to take care of us. So we decide to live at a 60 or 70 percent level of trust and wonder why we are so bored, frustrated, and unfulfilled spiritually.

I'm convinced that our problems are at heart theological. We've never settled the question, What kind of God do we believe in? In biblical terms, we've never settled the question of whether we believe God really cares for us. We think He does, we hope He does, but many days we're not sure.

When you get right down to it, we're not sure about God: We can't quite bring ourselves to trust Him. Until we, by a conscious choice, settle the big question, What kind of God do I believe in? all lesser questions will go unanswered.

Here is the genius of biblical Christianity. God cares for me. And He proved it by sending His own Son to die for me. At the Cross the issue was settled for eternity. Any God who would sacrifice His own Son for a person like me must care for me. There's no other reason He would do such a thing.

When we come to God, we don't have to convince Him to hear us. We don't have to chant or shout or burn incense or ring bells or use a priest or offer a sacrifice. No, we come as His children, and He gladly hears us. We don't do anything to make God care. We begin and act from the assurance, rooted in history, that God cares for us. And it's on that basis that we can unload all our worries on Him.

*Lord Jesus, help me to discern the difference between honest concern and sinful worry. Show me how to cast my cares upon You lest I collapse under the weight of my own problems. Amen.*

———— ✳ ————

## A MOMENT'S REFLECTION

What are your top five worries/burdens/concerns right now? Who is better able to handle those things—you or God? If the answer is God, take time right now to roll your burdens on the Lord. If the answer is you, go back and read this entry again.

---
✳
---

# Ninety

# UNLIMITED LOVE: HAVING A HEART LIKE GOD'S

*As for the saints who are in the land, they are the glorious ones in whom is all my delight.*

Psalm 16:3

Satan loves it when Christians bicker. First we split hairs, then we split churches. This is a message we do well to heed. It is God's word to us, and we ignore this truth at our own peril.

Unity is a precious gift of the Spirit. It is to be prized, sought, and guarded at all costs. When it is lost, it is hard to regain. Behind this fact lies a truth for us to consider. Today's blessing doesn't guarantee tomorrow's success. I believe that Satan loves to attack churches when they are doing well. If Satan can't destroy from without, he'll attack from within. If he can't destroy the doctrine, he'll attack the moral life of the leaders. If he can't corrupt the moral life of the leaders, he'll attack the unity of the body.

The biblical concept of brotherly love comes from a word meaning "tender affection owed to those born from the same womb." It's easy to understand why the early Christians adopted this word to describe Christian love. All Christians have been "born of the same womb" through the new birth. To be born again means to receive new life through personal faith in Jesus Christ. It means to be "born from God's womb."

I have three brothers—Andy, Alan, and Ron. I am the second of four Pritchard brothers. We're all very different. We live in four different states—Illinois, Alabama, Mississippi, and Arkansas. We have different personalities, different habits and hobbies, different likes and dislikes. Yet one thing binds us together. We come from the same womb. That fact means that there is a special place in my heart for my brothers. Even if I haven't seen them for a long time, it's as if I last saw them yesterday. There is a bond between us that time and distance cannot break.

The same truth applies in the spiritual realm. Everyone who belongs to Jesus belongs to me. And I owe all of them tender affection and brotherly love.

Let us be clear about this. We are to love all true believers everywhere all the time. No qualifications, no reservations. That's hard because most of us have some inner qualifications. We don't like this group or that denomination. Maybe we're not comfortable with people who speak in tongues or with those who use a prayer book. We may even distrust people who have a different worship style than we do. Maybe we have some preferences regarding skin color or ethnic background.

The love of God through Christ is not limited—not by nation or ocean or tribe or tongue or custom or clothing or race or politics or creed or caste or any other human condition. When the love of God captures us, our hearts

298

will be as big as His—reaching to the ends of the earth.

> *Lord God, teach me to love as You love—with a heart as
> big as Yours—and with arms that reach out to embrace
> all Your children. Amen.*

—✳—

## A MOMENT'S REFLECTION

Why is unity so important in the local church? What
happens when a church loses its unity? Think of a step
you could take today to reach out to a Christian brother
or sister who comes from a different background.

Section Ten

# A GLIMPSE OF ETERNITY

*And I—in righteousness I will see your face; when I awake, I will be satisfied with seeing your likeness.*

Psalm 17:15

———— ✳ ————

# Ninety-One

# STABILITY:
# A SOLID FOUNDATION
# IN A SHAKY WORLD

*You have shaken the land and torn it open; mend its fractures, for it is quaking.*

Psalm 60:2

The day is coming when all the world will be shaken by God. That shaking will be greater than any earthquake. And in that final great day everything man-made will be destroyed. Only eternal things will remain.

I don't know if you've ever been in an earthquake. We don't have many in the Chicago area. When I lived in California, we had a small tremor one day. It happened while I was driving home from church at lunchtime. Suddenly the car started rocking. I looked outside and the street was rocking. I was scared to death. To me, an earthquake is the most terrifying natural disaster. If a tornado comes, at least you can head for cover. But what do you do if the very ground on which you stand gives way beneath you? Where do you go then?

The scientists say that someday a great earthquake will come again to California. They know it's coming, only they don't know when. The Bible also speaks of a major earthquake (Haggai 2:6–7). But God is talking about an earthquake greater than anything the scientists at Cal Tech ever dreamed about. When this one comes, the whole earth will be shaken apart, and everything in which men put their trust will be gone. Money and houses, lands and cars, buildings and wardrobes—all of it wiped out in one brief moment. If you can see it, feel it, touch it, smell it, it will all disappear. Suddenly, everything will be shaken apart and destroyed.

What will be left? Only those things that cannot be shaken. Eternal things. The things of the spirit. The Word of God. Your own soul.

God's Word is clear: Don't pin your hopes on the world system. It's going down for good. It can't last. It's going to crumble and fall. The whole world and everything in it will be destroyed. If you live for this world, in that day everything you live for will be nothing but dust.

Therefore, if you have some money, invest it for God. If you have some food, share it with the poor. If you have some clothes, give to those who have none. If you have some water, give it to the thirsty. If you have some time on your hands, spend it with the hurting. If you have some good news, give it to the lost.

God is saying something important to us. He is giving us an unshakable kingdom. It's ours. Guaranteed. Therefore, we can afford to share the things of this world with others. It can't last much longer anyway.

*Lord, save me from building my life around things that will one day disappear. Show me the things that will last forever. Amen.*

— ✳ —

## A MOMENT'S REFLECTION

Do you agree that this world won't last forever? How much of your life is spent dealing with things that will one day disappear? What have you done in the last twenty-four hours that will have eternal significance?

---

✳

---

# Ninety-Two

# MORTALITY:
# YOU WON'T LIVE FOREVER

*Teach us to number our days aright, that we may gain a heart of wisdom.*

Psalm 90:12

Earlier in Psalm 90 Moses reminded us that we all are creatures of dust (v. 3). From the dust we come, and to the dust we shall all return. As the hymn writer penned, we are "Frail children of dust, and feeble as frail." We are here today and gone tomorrow—"like the new grass of the morning" that springs up fresh and by evening it is dry and withered (vv. 5–6).

If all we are is dust in the wind, how can we find meaning in life? Recently I heard a well-known public figure say that in his mind we're all like pop bottles on a conveyor belt. We drop on the belt, ride a little way, and then we fall off the belt, only to be replaced by another bottle. Not a very uplifting view of life, is it? But it is partly true. From one perspective we show up at birth, grow up, get old, and then we die, apparently to be replaced by someone younger. Where is the dignity in that? Psalm 90:4 adds a crucial fact to the mix: "For a thousand years in your sight are like a day that has just gone by, or like a watch in the night." God stands above history. He and He alone provides a meaningful context for the few years we live on planet Earth. What seems so important to us is as nothing in the grand scheme of eternity. In his great hymn "Immortal, Invisible," Walter Chalmers Smith wrote this verse:

> To all life Thou givest, to both great and small;
> In all life Thou livest, the true life of all;
> We blossom and flourish, like leaves on the tree,
> Then wither and perish, but naught changeth Thee.

God's perspective is radically different from ours. He works across the centuries to accomplish His purposes. There is no reason to boast when we could wither away at any moment. As our family gathered for a meal late one December my wife said, "Let's thank God for all His blessings during this year." Our youngest son immediately spoke up and said, "The year's not over yet. One of us could die today." True, and that's exactly the point Moses was making.

Lest this seem morbid, remember that a healthy sense of your own mortality can help you make wise decisions. That's why we need to "number our days." Recently I tried to calculate how much longer I was going to live. As of this moment, I've lived 16,790 days—give or take a few. If I live no longer than my father, I'll live 20,440 days, which leaves me with 3,650 days—or approximately ten more years. But who knows? I may be gone before you read these words—or I may live forty more years. But I won't be here forever, so I'd best number my days and use each one to serve God while I can.

*Lord, teach me to number my days so that I might use them for Your glory. Help me to remember that I won't be here forever. Amen.*

## A MOMENT'S REFLECTION

Take a moment to calculate the number of days you have lived so far. Now take a guess as to how many more days you expect to live. What is the most eternally profitable way you can spend your remaining days?

# Ninety-Three

# AFTER DEATH: WHAT THEN?

*But you will die like mere men; you will fall like every other ruler.*

Psalm 82:7

How can we explain the universal fascination with the world beyond the grave? Is it not because death is so final? Whatever one thinks about the reports of "near-death" visions, death when it finally comes is irreversible. When you cross the line, there is no coming back from the other side. Death wins the battle every time. After the doctors have tried the latest wonder drug, after the best minds have pooled their wisdom, after the philosophers have done their best to explain that death is only a natural part of life, we come face-to-face with the ugly reality that someday we will all die. And that death —whether expected or accidental, whether comfortable or painful—will be the end of life as we have known it.

No wonder the human mind is drawn to the question, "What happens when we die?" In many ways it is the one remaining unanswered question. We know so much about so many things, but about life after death, we know so very little.

Every person must answer three great questions:

1. Where did I come from?
2. Why am I here?
3. Where am I going?

It is the third question that most grips the heart of man, for in one sense, the question "Where did I come from?" is yesterday's news and the question "Why am I here?" is one that we answer every day, but the third question takes us into the unseen future—into the unfolding years and decades.

What happens when we die? Is death the end of everything? Does man live for a few years and then simply vanish from the screen? Do we simply play our part and then shuffle off the stage into the misty obscurity of nothingness? Or is there something more, something beyond the great divide? Thousands of years ago Job spoke for the rest of us when he asked, "If a man dies, will he live again?" (Job 14:14).

In answering questions about life after death, we are left with only two sources to consult. Either we turn to human experience or we turn to the Word of God. If we turn to human experience, we find many guesses, many ideas, many theories—but no sure answers. That's because, in the nature of the case, no human has a sure answer. The only people who have the answer are dead. That leaves us with the Word of God. In the Bible we find abundant answers. God who knows the future knows what happens when we die, and He hasn't left us to wonder about it. If you want the answer in one sentence, what happens after you die depends on what happens before you die.

> *Lord, since I am going to live forever somewhere, I pray to be prepared to spend eternity with You. Amen.*

— ✳ —

## A MOMENT'S REFLECTION

Picture the moment of your own death. How do you expect it will happen? Do you fear that moment? Describe what will happen to you the first five minutes after your death.

---
✳
---

# Ninety-Four

# LOYAL LOVE: WHY WE'RE NOT AFRAID TO DIE

*Give thanks to the Lord, for he is good. His love endures forever.*

Psalm 136:1

The call came at 7:30 Friday morning. A dear friend had died. The end came swiftly. He labored in breathing for about an hour. Then he took two or three breaths and he was gone. He always said he would fight to the end but that he wouldn't drag it out. It happened just as he predicted. I got to the house about 8:20 to spend some time with his wife. There was sorrow but also peace and a sense of relief. She told me that the night before some friends had come by to talk with her husband. The conversation focused on the topic of heaven. They talked about how wonderful heaven is and how good it is to know that you are going there. They didn't know that in just a few hours my friend would be there.

Jesus told us all about heaven when He said, "In my Father's house are many rooms; if it were not so, I would have told you. I am going there to prepare a place for you. And if I go and prepare a place for you, I will come back and take you to be with me that you also may be where I am" (John 14:2–3). Do you know the most important phrase in that passage? "If it were not so, I would have told you." Our Lord wouldn't lie about a thing like that. He always tells the truth. And when we stand by the grave of a fellow believer, we have to know the truth: Is death the end, or is there something else? "If it were not so, I would have told you."

Each verse of Psalm 136 contains the answering chorus: "His love endures forever." The phrase contains six Hebrew syllables—meant to be chanted out loud—that remind us by their repetition that all things show us God's love at work on behalf of His children.

The word for "love" refers to the loyal love of a covenant relationship, such as the loyalty of a husband to his wife, a father to his children, or a soldier to his country. God's love is eternal because His covenant is eternal. He cannot not love His people.

But the thought is more than God's love alone. The Hebrew word emphasizes the fact that God's love endures. It outlasts all the problems of life. It goes beyond the troubles we all face every day. It endures when our life comes to an end. We live and die, but God's love endures forever.

What gives us the confidence to face death with our heads held high? How can we cross the Jordan to reach the other side? We can because "his love endures forever." That's our hope. We die, but His love endures forever. We fail, but His love endures forever. We stumble and fall, but His love endures forever. We know it because

God has said it. We know it because Jesus has promised it. We know it because "his love endures forever."

*Eternal Lord, thank You for love that will not let me go. Amen.*

— ✳ —

## A MOMENT'S REFLECTION

If you died today, are you certain you would go to heaven? Do you think a person can ever be certain of such a thing? If you answer yes to the first two questions, what is the basis for your answer?

---
✳
---

# Ninety-Five

# THE LORD WILL RETURN: A REASON TO BE FAITHFUL

*Let those who love the Lord hate evil, for he guards the lives of his faithful ones and delivers them from the hand of the wicked.*

Psalm 97:10

Arthur Clarke gave Psalm 97 the title "Coming in the Clouds." The connection with the Second Coming of Christ seems apt since verses 1–6 call the earth to rejoice when His righteousness is finally revealed. Verse 7 warns of judgment to come on idolaters. Verses 8–9 declare that Israel will rejoice when the Lord, the Most High, reigns on the earth. The final three verses of this short psalm promise deliverance for the faithful and light for the righteous who are called upon to praise the name of the Lord.

Perhaps the most striking fact about this psalm is that the writer (who is not named) used the past tense, yet he spoke of events future to him (and to us). That is, he wrote with such certainty about the Second Coming that it was as if it had already happened.

Someday soon the Lord will return to the earth. But how soon is soon? Nearly three thousand years have passed since Psalm 97 was written, and two thousand years have passed since Jesus walked on the earth. No wonder skeptics cry out, "Where is the promise of his coming?" (2 Peter 3:4 KJV). Yet they forget that a day with the Lord is like a thousand years and a thousand years is like a day.

The people who scoffed at Noah later drowned when water covered the whole earth. No doubt they laughed about "nutty Noah" and his "crazy boat," but when the rains came down, the door was closed and they had nowhere else to turn. In the days of Noah, unbelievers went merrily about their daily business. They were eating and drinking, marrying and giving in marriage until the very day when Noah entered the ark (Matthew 24:37–39). Suddenly they were swept away by the rising floodwaters. Something similar will happen when Christ returns for His faithful people. They will be saved, but the wicked will be swept away.

That day is coming—and we pray it will come soon. All the signs point in that direction. But whether Christ comes today or tomorrow or not for a thousand years, God's promise is certain. Christ will return to the earth and will reign from David's throne in Jerusalem. No matter how long we have to wait, let's stay faithful to the Lord. Christ will return, and the scoffers will be silenced forever.

*Lord Jesus, more than anything else, I want to hear You say, "Well done, good and faithful servant." Help me to stay strong when others mock my faith. Amen.*

———✳———

## A MOMENT'S REFLECTION

Why is faithfulness so important to God? How does God reward faithfulness in this life? In the life to come?

# Ninety-Six

# RAISED IMMORTAL: OUR FUTURE DESTINY

*Therefore my heart is glad and my tongue rejoices; my body also will rest secure, because you will not abandon me to the grave, nor will you let your Holy One see decay.*

Psalm 16:9–10

What happens to believers the moment they die? Here is God's answer: Those who have trusted Jesus Christ as Savior go immediately into the presence of the Lord. They are "away from the body" and "at home with the Lord" (2 Corinthians 5:8). As the apostle Paul languished in a Roman jail, he expressed a desire to depart from his earthly body and its troubles and to be with Christ in heaven. In his mind, dying would be "gain" because it would usher him into the personal presence of Jesus Christ (Philippians 1:21–23). Jesus made the same promise to the thief on the cross: "Today you will be with me in paradise" (Luke 23:43).

Meanwhile the body is buried awaiting the day of resurrection. That's what David meant when he declared that God would not abandon him to the grave forever. Peter applied this verse to Christ's resurrection in Acts 2:31–32. Since our resurrection is linked with Christ's, these words of David apply directly to us. Because Christ arose, we too shall someday rise from the dead.

Often while conducting a graveside service I remind those present of the words God said to Moses when he heard the voice coming from the burning bush: "Take off your sandals, for the place where you are standing is holy ground" (Exodus 3:5). Then I will say something like this: "This place of burial is holy ground. Look around you. Today all you see are signs of death. Gravestones, markers, flowers, monuments. Everything about this place is quiet, peaceful, serene. It is a good place to bury the dead. But it won't always be like this. When Jesus returns this very spot will be a place of resurrection. Take off your shoes; you are standing on resurrection ground."

Ponder the implications of this truth. All the believers in Christ will be raised. That includes people who died two thousand years ago, like James and John and Peter, and believers who died fifteen hundred years ago, five hundred years ago, one hundred years ago, fifty years ago, ten years ago, one year ago, one month ago, and those who died in Christ this week. It includes Martin Luther, John Calvin, Peter Lombard, Charles Spurgeon, D. L. Moody, Billy Sunday, and Jim Elliot.

It will be a literal resurrection from the dead. How? We simply do not know. But the same God who raised Jesus from the dead will also raise all who follow Him. This includes those who die at sea, those whose bodies are cremated, those who die on the battlefield, and those who die a lingering death from cancer. They will be raised indestructible with brand-new bodies, clothed with immortality, healed, restored, put in their right minds, raised to live forever, raised to die no more.

Let the people of God rejoice. The grave will not have the final victory because the dead in Christ rise first.

*Rock of Ages, place before my eyes the glorious prospect of future resurrection and fill me with such heavenly longing that the world can have no hold on me. Amen.*

—— ✳ ——

## A MOMENT'S REFLECTION

Do you believe in the resurrection of the dead? Why is this doctrine absolutely essential to the Christian faith? Think of at least five names you could add to the list of believers now dead who will be raised when Christ returns.

---
✳
---

# Ninety-Seven

# JUDGMENT DAY: YOU CAN'T ESCAPE IT!

*Surely you will reward each person according to what he has done.*

Psalm 62:12

Here is a truth you can't escape: A day of judgment is coming for the human race. Hebrews 9:27 tells us that "Man is destined to die once, and after that to face judgment." That statement, as simple as it might seem, is desperately needed in our time, for we live in an age when men doubt that Judgment Day is coming. The watchword of the age is "If it's right for you, go ahead and do it." Most people today doubt that there is any such thing as absolute truth. All truth is relative, defined by the circumstances of time and place. Pilate's question resonates through the air—"What is truth?" (John 18:38) —and no one seems to be able to give an answer.

If you ask the average person on the street, "Do you believe in a universal day of judgment for the human race?" the answers you are likely to get will be something like, "I don't believe a God of love will judge anybody" or the old standby—"I'm not worried about it because I'm as good as the next fellow." The eternal optimist says, "I'll take my chances" while the positive thinker says, "Not to worry. I'm OK. You're OK. We're all OK."

David reminds us (in words quoted by Paul in Romans 2:6) that God has appointed a day in which He will judge the entire human race. Not as groups but as individuals ("each person"). The "reward" of that day will not always be positive, because it will be based on what each person has done.

Why are your works so important? Simply because your works reveal what is in your heart. Whatever is inside must eventually come out. This is a great principle that reveals itself in many ways. If you are angry inside, that anger must eventually reveal itself. If you are bitter, that bitterness will bubble to the surface. If you are a greedy person, your greed will show itself in your actions. If you are a bigot, you can't hide your bigotry forever. If you are a chattering fool, soon enough you'll open your mouth and prove it to the world. Likewise, if you are merciful, mercy will come forth. If you are gentle, the world will soon see your gentleness. If you are thrifty or wise or trustworthy or loving or a peacemaker . . . whatever you are on the inside will be seen in the way you live.

That's why God judges by works. Not to establish the way of salvation but the basis of judgment. You are saved by faith and judged by works. Is there a contradiction? Not at all. Your works ultimately reveal what is in your heart—either faith leading to life or unbelief leading to judgment.

*Righteous Judge, give me such grace that there may be no contradiction between my works and my faith. Amen.*

— ✳ —

## A MOMENT'S REFLECTION

How would you answer Pilate's question, "What is truth?" How do you respond to the person who says, "We're all going to heaven anyway"? In what sense do your works reveal the contents of your heart?

—————— ✳ ——————

# Ninety-Eight

# JERUSALEM: THE CITY GOD LOVES

*Pray for the peace of Jerusalem: "May those who love you be secure."*

Psalm 122:6

The King James Version says, "They shall prosper that love thee." God promises both peace and security to those who love the city of Jerusalem.

How strange that the "City of Peace" should require that its pilgrims pray for peace. Jerusalem, the City of Peace, has known very little peace. It has been destroyed and rebuilt forty-seven times. The Jerusalem of Jesus' day is seven to seventy feet below the level of the modern city.

For security reasons Jerusalem was always a walled city. The current walls were built by Suleiman the Magnificent in the 1600s. They were built on the old Byzantine walls, which are built on the remains of the Roman walls, which are built on the remains on the walls of Herod's temple, which was destroyed in A.D. 70 by the Roman army.

I have visited Jerusalem three times. Each time I go there, I am struck by two things:

1. Jerusalem is truly the "center of the world."
2. Jerusalem has known very little peace.

The current headlines speak of impending peace in the Middle East. Would that it were so. During my most recent visit to Jerusalem, I heard sirens blaring in the night as the police went from place to place. Everywhere we went we saw police, soldiers, and roadblocks. Soldiers are on duty throughout old Jerusalem. It took us two hours to go through customs and security at Ben Gurion Airport outside Tel Aviv—the tightest security in the world.

No, there is no peace in Jerusalem. So it is and so it has been for thousands of years.

As our tour group prepared to leave the Garden Tomb, I met the general secretary of the Garden Tomb Association. I thanked him for making such a place available so near the Old City of Jerusalem, and I told him that we had had a wonderful time with the Lord. I also told him we would be back again.

He thanked me with British dignity and wished us a good time during our remaining days in Jerusalem. His last words to me, spoken with solemn intensity, were, "Pray for the peace of Jerusalem."

He was saying the same thing King David did when he wrote this psalm three thousand years ago. Let us keep our eyes on Jerusalem, for it is the truly the center of the world. When Jesus returns, He will reign from David's throne in Jerusalem for one thousand years. As we rush headlong toward the end of this age, keep your Bible in one hand and your daily newspaper in the other. If you ever have the opportunity, visit the Holy City and rejoice with those who say, "Let us go to the house of the Lord." Above all else, in these troubled times, pray for the peace of Jerusalem.

*Lord Jesus, You loved the city of Jerusalem when You were on the earth. Come quickly, Lord Jesus, and establish the New Jerusalem where peace shall reign forever. Amen.*

— ✳ —

## A MOMENT'S REFLECTION

Why is this city so important in biblical history? Read Matthew 23:37–39 to see how Jesus felt about the city where He was crucified. Take a moment and pray for the peace of Jerusalem.

# Ninety-Nine

# ZION:
# OUR ETERNAL HOME

*The Lord loves the gates of Zion more than all the dwellings of Jacob.*

Psalm 87:2

Originally Mount Zion was the name of the hill on which the city of Jerusalem was built. Later Zion became the name of Jerusalem itself. Every time Zion is mentioned, it is the earthly dwelling place of God. In the Old Testament, the Jews would come marching to Zion, the city of Jerusalem, and there they would meet their God. By the time of the New Testament, Zion came to represent heaven, the eternal dwelling place of God. Everything we think of when we think about heaven is part of what the New Testament calls Zion. As in the Old Testament, there was a physical Zion and a physical city called Jerusalem, so in the New Testament there is a spiritual Mount Zion and a heavenly Jerusalem.

Hebrews 12:22 says, "But you have come to Mount Zion." The word the author used for "come" means to draw near, to come alongside. As Christians, we have drawn near to heaven. In Jesus Christ, we have come near to ultimate spiritual reality. There is more to the universe than meets the eye. The realm of spiritual reality cannot be measured in a test tube. Did you know there are thousands of voices all around you? Maybe tens of thousands. Where are they? Why can't you hear them? The voices are on radio waves from all over the world talking in dozens of languages. Add to that television signals, microwave phone signals, and satellite transmissions surrounding you on every side. We cannot see them or hear them because we aren't tuned in to the right frequency. But no one doubts they are there.

In Jesus Christ, we have come near to God and to heaven and to heavenly reality. Jesus introduced us to the throne room of the universe. Every time we pray, we have come near to God. Every time we worship together, heaven is not far away. Every time we sing a Christian song, we draw near to the angels. We are in God's presence, surrounded by angels, enrolled in heaven, accepted by God, not far from our loved ones, forgiven by the blood. We have something wonderful in Jesus. We live next door to heaven. All the unseen world is open to us. Not sometimes, but all the time. When we are tempted to go back to the old life, we remember that we have something infinitely greater at our disposal—God and Jesus and the church and the angels and our loved ones and Mount Zion and heaven itself. We have come to Mount Zion. And we intend to stay there. Nothing could improve our position. The world has nothing better to offer.

*Heavenly Father, Your blessings are so great that all the gold and silver in the world is nothing in comparison with the things You have prepared for us. Help me to live as one made rich by Your grace. Amen.*

———❋———

## A MOMENT'S REFLECTION

Take a piece of paper and jot down at least seven blessings that are yours through Jesus Christ. What does it mean to you that "heaven is not far away"? Do you think people in heaven are aware of what happens on the earth?

—————— ✳ ——————

# OUR BLESSED HOPE:
# JESUS IS COMING AGAIN

*Blessed is he who comes in the name of the Lord. From the house of the Lord we bless you.*

Psalm 118:26

This verse is quoted in all four gospels in connection with Christ's Triumphal Entry into Jerusalem. All four gospel writers make a point to mention what the people shouted. They specifically mention two things: First the people cried out, "Hosanna! Hosanna! Hosanna!" and second they said, "Blessed is he who comes in the name of the Lord." "Hosanna!" is a Hebrew word meaning "Save us now." As one writer put it, "Hosanna!" was a kind of "Holy Hurrah." Every observant Jew immediately recognized the second statement as a quotation from Psalm 118. They all knew it because Psalm 118 was one of the best-known Messianic psalms. By shouting these words, the people were in effect explicitly identifying Jesus as the promised Messiah. No other meaning could reasonably be construed from their exultant shouts. These people believed that at long last the Messiah had come.

They were right. The Messiah had come—in person, riding on the foal of a donkey. Sometimes it is overlooked that Jesus gladly accepted the praise of the people on

Palm Sunday. What a change this was. For most of His public ministry, whenever He worked a miracle, He told people not to spread the word. He wanted people to see Him as more than a miracle worker. But not that day. The time for silence was long past. If He once discouraged publicity, He now counted silence inconceivable. The time for truth had come. When the Pharisees heard the crowds praising Him, they urged Him to rebuke His disciples. Jesus refused, saying, "If I tell them to be quiet, the rocks themselves will break forth in praise to me."

Later that week, as His crucifixion drew near, Jesus confronted the Pharisees about their utter hypocrisy. After pronouncing seven "woes" upon them, He declared that Jerusalem would not see Him again until the people say, "Blessed is he who comes in the name of the Lord" (Matthew 23:39). Here is a solemn reminder of history's greatest mistake. The King had come to His people, and His people had put Him to death. But there is also in these words an implicit promise—"You will see Me again."

Thank God, the bloody cross is not the end of the story, nor does it end at the empty tomb or even with Jesus' visible ascension into heaven. If words have any meaning, Jesus promised to return to the same earth that had rejected Him. He came once as the Lamb of God; He will return as the Lion of the Tribe of Judah. And in that day, the nation of Israel will see Him as He is, and "all Israel will be saved" (Romans 11:26). That day is yet future to us, and no one can say when it will come. May it be soon. Even so, come Lord Jesus.

*Lord Jesus, You promised to return. Today wouldn't be too soon. If not today, then tomorrow. Help me to live so that I won't be surprised or ashamed when that glad day finally arrives. Amen.*

## A MOMENT'S REFLECTION

Do you expect Jesus to return in your lifetime? In what ways is the Second Coming the "blessed hope" of the believer? Are you ready for His return?

# SPECIAL NOTE

If you would like to contact the author, you can reach him in the following ways:

By Letter:        Ray Pritchard
Calvary Memorial Church
931 Lake Street
Oak Park, IL 60301

By phone: (708) 386-3900
By e-mail: PastorRay@cmcop.org
Via the Internet: www.cmcop.org

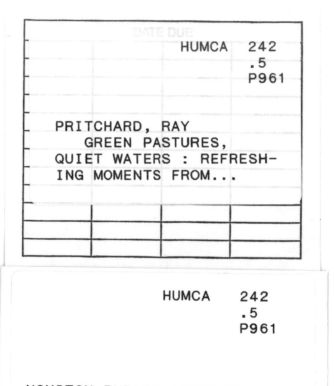